# MEDITERRANEAN
## COOKING

pil

Publications International, Ltd.

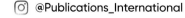

**Let's get social!**
 @Publications_International
 @PublicationsInternational
**www.pilbooks.com**

# CONTENTS

# WHAT IS THE MEDITERRANEAN LIFESTYLE?

The Mediterranean lifestyle or eating plan is a mostly commonsense approach modeled on the eating habits of countries that border the Mediterranean Sea. These include European countries: Spain, France, Italy and Greece; Middle Eastern countries: Turkey, Syria and Lebanon; and African countries: Egypt, Libya, Tunisia, Algeria and Morocco. Research that goes back as far as the 1950s indicates that people in these countries were exceptionally healthier and had lower risk to many lifestyle diseases, like heart attacks, strokes, type 2 diabetes, and obesity than Americans, based on their eating patterns and cooking styles.

This diverse list of countries may not seem to have much in common at first and people in each country consumes different foods, but as studies examine the native cuisines of the people, a pattern emerges focusing on a plant-food based diet and relatively low amount of animal foods with an emphasis on fresh vegetables, fruit, whole grains, fish and seafood, healthy unsaturated fats, and smaller amounts of meat, dairy and refined grains.

## BASIC COMPONENTS OF THE MEDITERRANEAN LIFESTYLE

**WHAT TO EAT:** a large variety of plant-based foods, including fruits (as desserts), vegetables, potatoes, whole grains, beans, nuts, legumes and seeds

**MOSTLY:** Vegetables, fruits, nuts, seeds, legumes, potatoes, whole grains, breads, herbs, spices, fish, seafood, extra virgin olive oil

**MODERATELY:** poultry (no more than twice/week) and fish, eggs (no more than 7/week, including those used in cooking), cheese, yogurt

**RARELY:** red meat (no more than twice/month)

**AVOID:** added sugars and sweets like candies, cookies, pastries, sweetened beverages, processed meats like hot dogs, sausages, refined grains and pasta, trans fats found in margarine and processed foods

**ACTIVITY:** include daily physical activity and positive lifestyle choices

## FOODS TO CHOOSE

**VEGETABLES:** tomatoes, broccoli, kale, spinach, onions, cauliflower, carrots, Brussels sprouts, eggplant, cucumbers, potatoes, sweet potatoes

**FRUITS:** apples, bananas, oranges, pears, berries, grapes, figs, dates, melons, peaches

**NUTS/SEEDS:** almonds, walnuts, macadamia nuts, hazelnuts, cashews, sunflower seeds, pumpkin seeds

**LEGUMES:** beans, peas, lentils, pulses, peanuts, chickpeas

**WHOLE GRAINS:** oats, brown rice, rye, barley, corn, buckwheat, whole wheat, whole grain pasta

**FISH/SEAFOOD:** salmon, sardines, trout, tuna, mackerel, shrimp, oysters, clams, crab, mussels

**POULTRY:** chicken, turkey, duck

**EGGS:** pasteurized or omega-3 enriched eggs

**DAIRY:** cheese, yogurt, particularly Greek yogurt

**HEALTHY FATS:** extra virgin olive oil, olives, avocados, avocado oil

**SPICES/CONDIMENTS:** garlic, cinnamon, turmeric, sea salt, pepper

**BEVERAGES:** water, red wine (limit to 1 glass daily), coffee, tea

**SNACKS:** nuts, fresh fruit or vegetables, Greek yogurt, hummus

## IDEAS FOR INCORPORATING THE MEDITERRANEAN APPROACH INTO YOUR LIFESTYLE

- Add vegetables to pastas, stir fries, soups
- Add beans/chickpeas to salads, quesadillas, tacos
- Add pine nuts or slivered almonds to green beans or other vegetables or rice
- Create trail mixes from dried fruits, whole-grain cereals, nuts and seeds
- Serve dips, like hummus (chickpea spread), tzatziki (yogurt-based dip) or baba ghanoush (eggplant and sesame) with vegetables and whole grain crackers

Overall, there is no one defined Mediterranean eating style. It's important to choose a plan that is rich in plant foods and lower in animal products and emphasize fish and seafood.

# STARTERS & SNACKS

## OLIVE HERB PULL-APARTS

**MAKES 10 SERVINGS**

2½ tablespoons extra virgin olive oil, divided

4 cloves garlic, minced

1 package (12 ounces) refrigerated buttermilk biscuits (10 biscuits)

¼ teaspoon red pepper flakes

1 red onion, very thinly sliced

½ cup shredded or chopped fresh basil

½ (2¼-ounce) can sliced black olives, drained

2 teaspoons chopped fresh rosemary

¼ cup (1 ounce) crumbled feta cheese

1. Preheat oven to 400°F. Line large baking sheet with parchment paper or spray with nonstick cooking spray.

2. Combine 1½ tablespoons oil and garlic in small bowl. Separate biscuits; arrange on baking sheet about ½ inch apart.* Lightly spray with olive oil cooking spray; let stand 10 minutes.

3. Flatten biscuits. Sprinkle with red pepper flakes, gently pressing into biscuits. Brush with garlic oil; top with onion.

4. Combine basil, olives, rosemary and remaining 1 tablespoon oil in small bowl. Spread mixture over biscuits; sprinkle with feta cheese.

5. Bake 10 minutes or until golden brown. Serve warm or at room temperature.

*For attractive presentation, place four biscuits in a line down center of baking sheet. Arrange half of remaining biscuits on each side.*

# LAVASH CHIPS WITH ARTICHOKE PESTO

MAKES 6 SERVINGS (ABOUT 1½ CUPS PESTO)

- 3 pieces lavash bread, each 7½×9½ inches
- ¼ cup plus 2 tablespoons olive oil, divided
- ¾ teaspoon kosher salt, divided
- 1 can (14 ounces) artichoke hearts, rinsed and drained
- ½ cup chopped walnuts, toasted*
- ¼ cup packed fresh basil leaves
- 1 clove garlic, minced
- 2 tablespoons lemon juice
- ¼ cup grated Parmesan cheese

*To toast walnuts, spread on baking sheet. Bake in preheated 350°F oven 6 to 8 minutes or until golden brown, stirring frequently.

1. Preheat oven to 350°F. Line two baking sheets with parchment paper. Position two oven racks in upper third and lower third of oven.

2. Brush both sides of each piece lavash with 2 tablespoons oil. Sprinkle with ¼ teaspoon salt. Bake 10 minutes or until lavash is crisp and browned, turning and rotating baking sheets between upper and lower racks after 5 minutes. Remove from oven; set on wire rack to cool completely.

3. Place artichoke hearts, walnuts, basil, garlic, lemon juice and remaining ½ teaspoon salt in food processor; pulse about 12 times until coarsely chopped. While food processor is running, slowly stream remaining ¼ cup oil until smooth. Add Parmesan cheese and pulse until blended.

4. Break lavash into chips. Serve with pesto.

# KASHK-E BADEMJAN (PERSIAN EGGPLANT DIP)

MAKES 12 TO 16 SERVINGS

3 large eggplants (3½ pounds total), peeled and cut into 1-inch cubes

1 teaspoon salt

5 tablespoons extra virgin olive oil, divided

2 onions, chopped

1 tablespoon dried mint

3 tablespoons plain nonfat Greek yogurt

⅓ cup finely chopped walnuts

Pita bread and/or assorted vegetable sticks

## SLOW COOKER DIRECTIONS

1. Toss eggplant cubes with salt in large bowl; transfer to large colander. Place colander in large bowl or sink; let stand 1 hour at room temperature to drain.

2. Meanwhile, heat 1 tablespoon oil in large nonstick skillet over medium-high heat. Add onions; cook 5 to 6 minutes or until lightly browned, stirring occasionally. Transfer to slow cooker. Stir in eggplant. Cover; cook on LOW 6 to 8 hours or on HIGH 3½ to 4 hours or until eggplant is very soft.

3. Heat remaining 4 tablespoons oil in small saucepan over low heat. Add mint; cook about 15 minutes or until very fragrant. Set aside to cool slightly.

4. Transfer eggplant and onions to colander or fine mesh strainer with slotted spoon; press out any excess liquid with back of spoon. Return to slow cooker; mash with fork. Stir in yogurt. Sprinkle with chopped walnuts; drizzle with mint oil. Serve warm with pita bread and/or assorted vegetable sticks.

TIP: Traditionally this dish is made with Kashk, an Iranian dairy product similar to sour cream and whey. Thick Greek-style strained yogurt is the closest substitute that is widely available in U.S. markets. "Bademjan" is the word for "eggplant" in Farsi, a language spoken in Iran.

# SPINACH, ARTICHOKE AND FETA DIP

MAKES 6 SERVINGS (ABOUT 1½ CUPS)

½ cup thawed frozen chopped spinach

1 cup (4 ounces) crumbled feta cheese

½ teaspoon black pepper

1 cup marinated artichokes, undrained

Pita chips, cucumber slices and/or bell pepper strips

1. Place spinach in small microwavable bowl; microwave on HIGH 2 minutes.

2. Place feta cheese and pepper in food processor. Process 1 minute or until finely chopped. Add artichokes and spinach; process 30 seconds until well mixed but not puréed. Serve with pita chips or vegetables.

# CROSTINI WITH EGGPLANT TAPENADE

MAKES 8 SERVINGS

- 3 tablespoons olive oil
- 2 cups diced eggplant
- ⅓ cup diced shallots or onion
- 1 cup pitted kalamata olives, chopped
- 1 tablespoon capers
- ½ cup red peppadew peppers, chopped with 2 tablespoons juice*
- ½ cup cola beverage
- 1 tablespoon balsamic vinegar
- ½ teaspoon red pepper flakes
- Salt and black pepper
- Toasted baguette slices

*If peppadew peppers are unavailable, substitute chopped roasted red peppers.

1. Heat oil in large nonstick skillet over medium-high heat. Add eggplant and shallots; cook about 6 minutes or until richly golden, stirring often. Add olives, capers and peppadew peppers with juice; cook and stir 5 minutes or until most liquid has evaporated.

2. Stir in cola, vinegar, red pepper flakes, salt and black pepper. Reduce heat to low; cook about 15 minutes or until thickened, stirring occasionally. Serve warm or at room temperature on baguette slices.

TIP: This versatile eggplant tapenade can also be served on top of crackers or with raw crudités.

# ROASTED GARLIC HUMMUS

**MAKES 6 SERVINGS**

- 2 tablespoons Roasted Garlic (recipe follows)
- 1 can (about 15 ounces) chickpeas, rinsed and drained
- ¼ cup sprigs fresh parsley
- 2 tablespoons water
- 2 tablespoons lemon juice
- ½ teaspoon curry powder
- ⅛ teaspoon dark sesame oil
- Dash hot pepper sauce (optional)
- Pita bread wedges and fresh vegetables (optional)

1. Prepare Roasted Garlic.

2. Place chickpeas, parsley, 2 tablespoons Roasted Garlic, water, lemon juice, curry powder, sesame oil and hot pepper sauce, if desired, in food processor or blender. Cover; process until smooth.

3. Serve with pita wedges and vegetables, if desired.

ROASTED GARLIC: Cut off top third of 1 large garlic head (not the root end) to expose cloves; discard top. Place head of garlic, trimmed end up, on 10-inch square of foil. Rub garlic generously with olive oil and sprinkle with salt. Gather foil ends together and close tightly. Roast in preheated 350°F oven 45 minutes or until cloves are golden and soft. When cool enough to handle, squeeze roasted garlic cloves from skins; discard skins.

# SPANIKOPITA CUPS

MAKES 16 CUPS (8 SERVINGS)

- 6 tablespoons (¾ stick) butter, melted
- 2 eggs
- 1 container (15 ounces) ricotta cheese
- 1 package (10 ounces) frozen chopped spinach, thawed and squeezed dry
- 1 package (4 to 5 ounces) crumbled feta cheese
- ¾ teaspoon finely grated lemon peel
- ½ teaspoon salt
- ¼ teaspoon black pepper
- ⅛ teaspoon ground nutmeg
- 8 sheets frozen phyllo dough, thawed

1. Preheat oven to 350°F. Grease 16 standard (2½-inch) muffin pan cups with some of the butter.

2. Whisk eggs in large bowl. Add ricotta cheese, spinach, feta cheese, lemon peel, salt, pepper and nutmeg; whisk until well blended.

3. Place 1 sheet of phyllo on work surface. Brush with some of the butter; top with second sheet. Repeat layers twice. Cut stack of phyllo into eight rectangles; fit rectangles into prepared muffin cups, pressing into bottoms and up sides of cups. Repeat with remaining 4 sheets of phyllo and butter. Fill phyllo cups with spinach mixture.

4. Bake about 18 minutes or until phyllo is golden brown and filling is set. Cool in pans 2 minutes; remove to wire racks. Serve warm.

# BRUSCHETTA

MAKES 8 SERVINGS (1 CUP)

- **4** plum tomatoes, seeded and diced
- **½** cup packed fresh basil leaves, finely chopped
- **5** tablespoons olive oil, divided
- **2** cloves garlic, minced
- **2** teaspoons finely chopped oil-packed sun-dried tomatoes
- **¼** teaspoon salt
- **⅛** teaspoon black pepper
- **16** slices Italian bread
- **2** tablespoons grated Parmesan cheese

1. Combine plum tomatoes, basil, 3 tablespoons oil, garlic, sun-dried tomatoes, salt and pepper in large bowl; mix well. Let stand at room temperature 1 hour to blend flavors.

2. Preheat oven to 375°F. Place bread on baking sheet. Brush remaining 2 tablespoons oil over one side of bread slices; sprinkle with Parmesan cheese. Bake 6 to 8 minutes or until toasted.

3. Top each bread slice with 1 tablespoon tomato mixture.

# TZATZIKI CUCUMBER DIP WITH CRUDITÉS

MAKES 10 SERVINGS

### DIP

- 1 cup peeled diced English cucumber
- 2 cups plain Greek yogurt

  Freshly grated peel of 1 lemon
- 3 tablespoons fresh lemon juice
- 2½ tablespoons minced fresh mint
- 2 tablespoons extra virgin olive oil
- 1 tablespoon minced garlic
- 2 teaspoons sea salt
- 1½ teaspoons white wine vinegar

### CRUDITÉS

  Baby carrots

  Grape tomatoes

  Green onions, trimmed

  Zucchini, cut into 2×⅜-inch pieces

  Bell peppers, cut into 2×⅜-inch pieces

1. Wrap cucumber in clean dish towel. Twist towel to squeeze juice from cucumber; discard juice.

2. Combine cucumber, yogurt, lemon peel, lemon juice, mint, oil, garlic, salt and vinegar in medium bowl; mix well. Cover and refrigerate at least 2 hours.

3. Place dip in serving bowl. Serve with vegetables.

# CITRUS-MARINATED OLIVES

MAKES 16 SERVINGS (2 TABLESPOONS PER SERVING)

- 1 cup (about 8 ounces) large green olives, drained
- 1 cup kalamata olives, rinsed and drained
- ⅓ cup extra virgin olive oil
- ¼ cup orange juice
- 3 tablespoons sherry vinegar or red wine vinegar
- 2 tablespoons lemon juice
- 1 tablespoon grated orange peel
- 1 tablespoon grated lemon peel
- ½ teaspoon ground cumin
- ¼ teaspoon red pepper flakes

Combine all ingredients in medium glass bowl. Let stand overnight at room temperature. Refrigerate for up to 2 weeks.

# ANTIPASTO WITH MARINATED MUSHROOMS

MAKES 6 TO 8 SERVINGS

Marinated Mushrooms
(recipe follows)

4 teaspoons red wine
   vinegar

½ teaspoon dried basil

½ teaspoon dried oregano

⅛ teaspoon black pepper

¼ cup extra virgin olive oil

4 ounces mozzarella cheese,
   cut into ½-inch cubes

4 ounces prosciutto or
   cooked ham, thinly sliced

4 ounces provolone cheese,
   cut into 2-inch sticks

1 jar (10 ounces)
   pepperoncini peppers,
   drained

8 ounces hard salami, thinly
   sliced

2 jars (6 ounces each)
   marinated artichoke
   hearts, drained

6 ounces black olives

Fresh basil leaves or chives
   (optional)

1. Prepare Marinated Mushrooms; set aside. Combine vinegar, dried basil, oregano and black pepper in medium bowl. Add oil; whisk until well blended. Add mozzarella cubes; stir to coat. Marinate, covered, in refrigerator at least 2 hours.

2. Drain mozzarella cubes, reserving marinade. Wrap 1 prosciutto slice around each provolone stick.

3. Arrange mozzarella cubes, prosciutto-wrapped provolone sticks, Marinated Mushrooms, pepperoncini, salami, artichoke hearts and olives on large platter. Drizzle reserved marinade over artichoke hearts and olives. Garnish with fresh basil. Serve with small forks or toothpicks.

# MARINATED MUSHROOMS
MAKES ½ POUND

- 3 **tablespoons lemon juice**
- 2 **tablespoons chopped fresh parsley**
- 1 **clove garlic, crushed**
- ½ **teaspoon salt**
- ¼ **teaspoon dried tarragon**
- ⅛ **teaspoon black pepper**
- ½ **cup extra virgin olive oil**
- ½ **pound small or medium mushrooms, stems removed**

1. Combine lemon juice, parsley, garlic, salt, tarragon and black pepper in medium bowl. Add oil; whisk until well blended. Add mushrooms; stir to coat. Marinate, covered, in refrigerator 4 hours or overnight, stirring occasionally.

2. Drain mushrooms; reserve marinade for dressing.

# QUICK & EASY HUMMUS

MAKES 4 SERVINGS

1 clove garlic, peeled

1 can (about 15 ounces) chickpeas, rinsed and drained

2 tablespoons torn fresh mint leaves (optional)

2 tablespoons olive oil

2 tablespoons lemon juice

2 teaspoons dark sesame oil

½ teaspoon salt

⅛ teaspoon ground red pepper *or* ¼ teaspoon hot pepper sauce

With motor running, drop garlic clove through feed tube of food processor. Add remaining ingredients to food processor. Cover; process until hummus is well combined and is desired consistency (the longer the hummus is processed the smoother the texture).

SERVING SUGGESTION: Serve with vegetable dippers or pita bread.

TIP: Leftover hummus may be covered and refrigerated up to 1 week. Hummus makes a great sandwich spread for pita bread rounds.

# TIROKAFTERI (SPICY GREEK FETA SPREAD)

MAKES 2 CUPS

- 2 small hot red peppers
- ½ small clove garlic
- 1 block (8 ounces) feta cheese
- ¾ cup plain Greek yogurt
- 1 tablespoon lemon juice
- ½ teaspoon salt
- Sliced French bread, crostini, pita bread and/or cut-up vegetables

1. Preheat oven to 400°F. Place peppers on small piece of foil or baking sheet. Bake 15 minutes or until peppers are soft and charred. Cool completely. Scrape off skin with paring knife. Cut off top and remove seeds. Place peppers in food processor. Add garlic; pulse until finely chopped.

2. Add feta cheese, yogurt, lemon juice and salt; pulse until well blended but still chunky. Store in airtight jar in refrigerator up to 2 weeks. Serve with bread or vegetables.

# SPICY ROASTED CHICKPEAS

MAKES 8 (¼-CUP) SERVINGS

1 can (about 15 ounces) chickpeas, rinsed and drained

3 tablespoons olive oil

½ teaspoon salt

½ teaspoon black pepper

¾ to 1 tablespoon chili powder

⅛ to ¼ teaspoon ground red pepper

1 lime, cut into wedges

1. Preheat oven to 400°F.

2. Combine chickpeas, oil, salt and black pepper in large bowl; toss to coat. Spread in single layer on sheet pan.

3. Bake 15 minutes or until chickpeas begin to brown, shaking pan twice.

4. Sprinkle with chili powder and red pepper. Bake 5 minutes or until dark golden-red. Serve with lime wedges.

# MEDITERRANEAN BAKED FETA

MAKES 4 TO 6 SERVINGS

1 package (8 ounces) feta cheese, cut crosswise into 4 slices

½ cup grape tomatoes, halved

¼ cup sliced roasted red peppers

¼ cup pitted kalamata olives

⅛ teaspoon dried oregano

Black pepper

2 tablespoons extra virgin olive oil

1 tablespoon shredded fresh basil

Pita chips

1. Preheat oven to 400°F.

2. Place feta cheese in small baking dish; top with tomatoes, roasted peppers and olives. Sprinkle with oregano and season with black pepper; drizzle with oil.

3. Bake 12 minutes or until cheese is soft. Sprinkle with basil. Serve immediately with pita chips.

# BREAKFAST & BRUNCH

## PEPPER AND EGG COUSCOUS BOWL

MAKES 4 SERVINGS

1 tablespoon olive oil

3 bell peppers, assorted colors, thinly sliced

1 red onion, thinly sliced

2 cups vegetable broth

1 cup uncooked instant couscous

1 clove garlic, minced

½ teaspoon salt

½ teaspoon dried oregano

½ teaspoon ground cumin

4 to 8 eggs, cooked any style

1 can (about 15 ounces) black beans, rinsed and drained

1 cup grape tomatoes, halved

Crumbled queso fresco, cotija or feta cheese (optional)

1. Heat oil in large skillet over medium-high heat. Add bell peppers and onion; cook and stir 5 minutes or until vegetables are tender.

2. Bring broth to a boil in small saucepan. Stir in couscous, garlic, salt, oregano and cumin. Remove from heat. Cover and let stand 5 minutes. Fluff with fork.

3. Serve vegetables, eggs and beans over couscous; top with tomatoes and cheese, if desired.

# GREEK ISLES OMELET

**MAKES 2 SERVINGS**

¼ cup chopped onion

¼ cup canned artichoke hearts, rinsed, drained and sliced

¼ cup chopped fresh spinach

¼ cup chopped plum tomato

2 tablespoons sliced pitted black olives, rinsed and drained

1 cup cholesterol-free egg substitute *or* 4 eggs

Dash black pepper

1. Spray small nonstick skillet with nonstick cooking spray; heat over medium heat. Add onion; cook and stir 2 minutes or until crisp-tender. Add artichokes; cook and stir until heated through. Add spinach, tomato and olives; gently stir. Remove to small bowl.

2. Wipe out skillet with paper towels and spray with cooking spray. Whisk egg substitute and pepper in medium bowl until well blended. Heat skillet over medium heat. Pour egg mixture into skillet; cook and stir gently, lifting edge to allow uncooked portion to flow underneath. Cook just until set.

3. Spoon vegetable mixture over half of omelet; gently loosen omelet with spatula and fold in half. Cut in half; serve immediately.

# FABULOUS FETA FRITTATA

MAKES 4 SERVINGS

8 eggs

¼ cup chopped fresh basil

¼ cup whipping cream or half-and-half

¼ teaspoon salt

¼ teaspoon freshly ground black pepper

2 tablespoons butter or olive oil

1 package (4 ounces) crumbled feta cheese with basil, olives and sun-dried tomatoes *or* 1 cup crumbled feta cheese

¼ cup pine nuts

1. Preheat broiler.

2. Beat eggs, basil, cream, salt and pepper in medium bowl. Melt butter in large ovenproof skillet over medium heat, tilting skillet to coat bottom and side.

3. Pour egg mixture into skillet. Cover and cook 8 to 10 minutes or until eggs are set around edge (center will be wet).

4. Sprinkle feta cheese and pine nuts evenly over top. Transfer to broiler; broil 4 to 5 inches from heat source 2 minutes or until center is set and pine nuts are golden brown. Cut into wedges to serve.

TIP: If skillet is not ovenproof, wrap the handle in heavy-duty foil.

# MEDITERRANEAN SCRAMBLE PITAS

**MAKES 4 SERVINGS**

- 2 teaspoons canola oil, divided
- 1 cup sliced zucchini and/or yellow squash
- 1 cup diced green bell peppers
- 1 cup grape tomatoes, quartered
- ¼ teaspoon dried rosemary
- 12 small stuffed green olives, quartered
- ¼ cup finely chopped fresh Italian parsley
- 1 cup cholesterol-free egg substitute
- 2 multigrain pita bread rounds, halved and warmed
- ¼ cup (1 ounce) crumbled reduced-fat feta cheese

1. Heat 1 teaspoon oil in large nonstick skillet over medium-high heat. Add zucchini and bell peppers; cook 4 minutes or until crisp-tender. Add tomatoes and rosemary; cook 2 minutes, stirring frequently. Stir in olives and parsley. Place in medium bowl. Cover to keep warm.

2. Wipe out skillet with paper towel. Add remaining 1 teaspoon oil and heat over medium heat. Cook egg substitute until set, lifting edges to allow uncooked portion to flow underneath.

3. Fill each warmed pita half with equal amounts of eggs and feta cheese. Top with vegetable mixture.

# SUPER OATMEAL

MAKES 6 SERVINGS

2 cups water

2¾ cups old-fashioned oats

½ cup finely diced dried figs*

⅓ cup lightly packed dark brown sugar

⅓ to ½ cup sliced almonds, toasted**

¼ cup flaxseeds

½ teaspoon salt

½ teaspoon ground cinnamon

2 cups reduced-fat (2%) or whole milk, plus additional for serving

*Beige Turkish figs are preferred if your market carries them.

**To toast almonds, spread in single layer on baking sheet. Bake in preheated 350°F oven 8 to 10 minutes or until golden brown, stirring frequently.

1. Bring water to a boil in large saucepan over high heat. Stir in oats, figs, brown sugar, almonds, flaxseeds, salt and cinnamon. Immediately add 2 cups milk. Stir well.

2. Reduce heat to medium-high. Cook and stir 5 to 7 minutes or until oatmeal is thick and creamy. Spoon into individual bowls. Serve with additional milk, if desired.

# MEDITERRANEAN FRITTATA

**MAKES 6 SERVINGS**

- ¼ cup extra virgin olive oil
- 5 small onions, thinly sliced
- 1 can (about 14 ounces) whole tomatoes, drained and chopped
- ¼ pound prosciutto or cooked ham, chopped
- ¼ cup grated Parmesan cheese
- 2 tablespoons chopped fresh parsley
- ½ teaspoon dried marjoram
- ¼ teaspoon salt
- ¼ teaspoon dried basil
- ⅛ teaspoon black pepper
- 6 eggs
- 2 tablespoons butter

1. Heat oil in large skillet over medium-high heat. Add onions; cook and stir 8 to 10 minutes until soft and golden. Reduce heat to medium. Add tomatoes; cook 5 minutes. Remove vegetables to large bowl with slotted spoon; discard drippings. Cool to room temperature.

2. Stir prosciutto, Parmesan cheese, parsley, marjoram, salt, basil and pepper into tomato mixture. Whisk eggs in medium bowl; stir into prosciutto mixture.

3. Preheat broiler. Heat butter in medium broilerproof nonstick skillet over medium heat until melted and bubbly. Reduce heat to low; add egg mixture to skillet, spreading evenly. Cook 8 to 10 minutes until all but top ¼ inch of frittata is set. (Shake skillet gently to test.) *Do not stir.*

4. Broil frittata about 4 inches from heat 1 to 2 minutes or until top is set. (Do not brown or frittata will be dry.) Serve warm or at room temperature. Cut into wedges.

# SPINACH, MUSHROOM, EGG AND GRUYÈRE ROLLUPS

MAKES 4 SERVINGS

1 tablespoon plus
  4 teaspoons olive oil,
  divided

1 shallot, thinly sliced (about
  ½ cup)

1 package (6 ounces) fresh
  baby spinach

1 clove garlic, minced

½ teaspoon plus ⅛ teaspoon
  salt, divided

8 ounces cremini mushrooms,
  thinly sliced

¼ teaspoon black pepper,
  divided

2 pieces flatbread,
  9½×11-inches, lightly
  toasted

⅔ cup shredded Gruyère
  cheese

6 eggs

2 tablespoons milk

2 teaspoons Dijon mustard

1. Heat 2 teaspoons oil in large nonstick skillet over medium heat. Add shallot; cook 5 to 6 minutes until softened. Increase heat to medium-high, add spinach; cook 2 minutes until wilted. Add garlic and ¼ teaspoon salt; cook 1 minute, stirring frequently. Set aside.

2. Heat 1 tablespoon oil in same skillet over medium-high heat. Add mushrooms, ¼ teaspoon salt and ⅛ teaspoon pepper; cook 6 minutes until browned, stirring occasionally.

3. Place half of spinach-mushroom mixture on each flatbread; top with cheese.

4. Whisk eggs in large bowl. Add remaining ⅛ teaspoon salt, ⅛ teaspoon pepper, milk and mustard.

5. Heat remaining 2 teaspoons oil in same skillet over medium-high heat. Add egg mixture; cook about 1 minute, stirring frequently, until eggs are set but not dry.

6. Place cooked eggs on spinach; roll up flatbread. Cut on bias to serve.

TIP: Serve at room temperature or heat in microwave 5 to 10 seconds on HIGH to warm.

MAKE AHEAD: Prepare rollups ahead of time and reheat in microwave when ready to eat.

# ASPARAGUS FRITTATA PROSCIUTTO CUPS

MAKES 12 CUPS (6 SERVINGS)

1 tablespoon olive oil

1 small red onion, finely chopped

1½ cups sliced asparagus (½-inch pieces)

1 clove garlic, minced

12 thin slices prosciutto

8 eggs

½ cup (2 ounces) grated white Cheddar cheese

¼ cup grated Parmesan cheese

2 tablespoons milk

⅛ teaspoon black pepper

1. Preheat oven to 375°F. Spray 12 standard (2½-inch) muffin cups with nonstick cooking spray.

2. Heat oil in large skillet over medium heat. Add onion; cook and stir 4 minutes or until softened. Add asparagus and garlic; cook and stir 8 minutes or until asparagus is crisp-tender. Set aside to cool slightly.

3. Line each prepared muffin cup with prosciutto slice. (Prosciutto should cover cup as much as possible, with edges extending above muffin pan.) Whisk eggs, Cheddar and Parmesan cheeses, milk and pepper in large bowl until well blended. Stir in asparagus mixture until blended. Pour into prosciutto-lined cups, filling about three-fourths full.

4. Bake about 20 minutes or until frittatas are puffed and golden brown and edges are pulling away from pan. Cool in pan 10 minutes; remove to wire rack. Serve warm or at room temperature.

# MEDITERRANEAN ARTICHOKE OMELET

**MAKES 1 SERVING**

2 eggs

1 tablespoon grated Parmesan cheese

2 tablespoons olive oil

3 cans (14 ounces each) artichoke bottoms packed in water, drained and diced

1 ounce (about 2 pieces) roasted red peppers, diced

½ teaspoon minced garlic

1 tablespoon tomato salsa

1. Beat eggs well in small bowl. Stir in Parmesan cheese.

2. Heat oil in large skillet over medium-high heat. Add artichokes; cook and stir 2 to 3 minutes or until beginning to brown. Add roasted peppers; cook and stir 2 minutes or until liquid has evaporated. Add garlic; cook and stir 30 seconds. Remove to small plate; keep warm.

3. Add egg mixture to skillet. Lift edge of omelet with spatula to allow uncooked portion to flow underneath. Cook 1 to 2 minutes or until omelet is almost set.

4. Spoon artichoke mixture onto half of omelet; fold omelet over filling. Cook 2 minutes or until set. Serve with salsa.

NOTE: Raw eggs will turn green if combined with raw artichokes because of a chemical reaction between the two foods. Cooking the artichokes separately will prevent this from happening.

# LUNCH & LIGHTER FARE

## MEDITERRANEAN VEGETABLE SANDWICH

**MAKES 4 SANDWICHES**

½ cup plain hummus

½ jalapeño pepper, seeded and minced*

¼ cup minced fresh cilantro

8 slices whole wheat bread

4 leaves lettuce (leaf or Bibb lettuce)

2 tomatoes, thinly sliced

½ cucumber, thinly sliced

½ red onion, thinly sliced

½ cup thinly sliced peppadew peppers or sweet Italian peppers

4 tablespoons (1 ounce) crumbled feta cheese

*\*Jalapeño peppers can sting and irritate the skin, so wear rubber gloves when handling peppers and do not touch your eyes.*

1. Combine hummus, jalapeño pepper and cilantro in small bowl; mix well.

2. Spread about 1 tablespoon hummus mixture on one side of each bread slice. Layer half of bread slices with lettuce, tomatoes, cucumber, onion, peppadew peppers and feta cheese; top with remaining bread slices. Cut sandwiches in half to serve.

# SLOW-COOKED SHAKSHUKA

**MAKES 6 SERVINGS**

¼ cup extra virgin olive oil

1 medium onion, chopped

1 large red bell pepper, chopped

3 cloves garlic, sliced

1 can (28 ounces) crushed tomatoes with basil, garlic and oregano

2 teaspoons paprika

2 teaspoons ground cumin

2 teaspoons sugar

½ teaspoon salt

¼ teaspoon red pepper flakes

¾ cup (3 ounces) crumbled feta cheese

6 eggs

## SLOW COOKER DIRECTIONS

**1.** Spray inside of slow cooker with nonstick cooking spray. Combine oil, onion, bell pepper, garlic, tomatoes, paprika, cumin, sugar, salt and red pepper flakes in slow cooker. Cover; cook on HIGH 3 hours. Stir in feta cheese; break eggs, one at a time, onto top of tomato mixture, leaving small amount of space between each.

**2.** Cover; cook on HIGH 15 to 18 minutes or until the egg whites are set but yolks are still creamy. Scoop eggs and sauce evenly onto each serving dish.

# EGGPLANT CRÊPES WITH ROASTED TOMATO SAUCE

**MAKES 4 TO 6 SERVINGS**

Roasted Tomato Sauce
(recipe follows)

2 eggplants (about 8 to
9 inches long), cut into
18 (¼-inch-thick) slices

1 package (10 ounces)
frozen chopped spinach,
thawed and squeezed
dry

1 cup ricotta cheese

½ cup grated Parmesan
cheese

1¼ cups (5 ounces) shredded
Gruyère* cheese

Fresh oregano leaves
(optional)

*Gruyère cheese is a Swiss cheese
that has been aged for 10 to
12 months. Any Swiss cheese can
be substituted.*

**1.** Prepare Roasted Tomato Sauce. *Reduce oven temperature to 425°F.*

**2.** Arrange eggplant on nonstick baking sheets in single layer. Spray both sides of eggplant slices with nonstick olive oil cooking spray. Bake eggplant 10 minutes; turn and bake 5 to 10 minutes or until tender. Cool. *Reduce oven temperature to 350°F.*

**3.** Combine spinach, ricotta and Parmesan cheese; mix well. Spray 12×8-inch baking pan with cooking spray. Spread spinach mixture evenly on eggplant slices; roll up slices, beginning at short ends. Place rolls, seam-side down, in baking dish.

**4.** Cover dish with foil. Bake 25 minutes. Uncover; sprinkle rolls with Gruyère cheese. Bake, uncovered, 5 minutes or until cheese is melted.

**5.** Serve with Roasted Tomato Sauce. Garnish with oregano leaves.

# ROASTED TOMATO SAUCE

**MAKES ABOUT 1 CUP**

20 ripe plum tomatoes (about
2⅔ pounds), cut in half
and seeded

3 tablespoons olive oil,
divided

½ teaspoon salt

⅓ cup minced fresh basil

½ teaspoon black pepper

Preheat oven to 450°F. Toss tomatoes with 1 tablespoon oil and salt in large bowl. Place, cut sides down, on nonstick baking sheet. Bake 20 to 25 minutes or until skins are blistered. Cool. Process tomatoes, remaining 2 tablespoons oil, basil and pepper in food processor until smooth.

# LIGHT GREEK SPANAKOPITA

**MAKES 4 SERVINGS**

1 teaspoon olive oil

1 large onion, cut into quarters and sliced

2 cloves garlic, minced

1 package (10 ounces) frozen chopped spinach, thawed and squeezed dry

½ cup (2 ounces) crumbled reduced-fat feta cheese

5 sheets phyllo dough, thawed*

½ cup cholesterol-free egg substitute

¼ teaspoon ground nutmeg

¼ to ½ teaspoon black pepper

⅛ teaspoon salt

*Thaw entire package of phyllo dough overnight in refrigerator.*

1. Preheat oven to 375°F. Spray 8-inch square baking pan with nonstick olive oil cooking spray.

2. Heat oil in large skillet over medium heat. Add onion; cook and stir 7 to 8 minutes or until soft. Add garlic; cook and stir 30 seconds. Add spinach and feta cheese; cook and stir until spinach is heated through. Remove from heat.

3. Place 1 sheet phyllo dough on counter with long side toward you. (Cover remaining sheets with damp towel until needed.) Spray right half of phyllo with cooking spray; fold left half over sprayed half. Place sheet in prepared pan. (Two edges will hang over sides of pan.) Spray top of sheet. Spray and fold 2 more sheets of phyllo the same way. Place sheets in pan at 90° angles so edges will hang over all four sides of pan. Spray each sheet after it is placed in pan.

4. Combine egg substitute, nutmeg, pepper and salt in small bowl. Stir into spinach mixture until blended. Spread filling over phyllo in pan. Spray and fold 1 sheet phyllo as above; place on top of filling, tucking ends under filling. Bring all overhanging edges of phyllo over top sheet; spray lightly. Spray and fold last sheet as above; place over top sheet, tucking ends under. Spray lightly. Bake 25 to 27 minutes or until top is barely browned. Cool 10 to 15 minutes before serving.

# MEDITERRANEAN FLATBREAD

**MAKES 16 PIECES**

- 2 tablespoons olive oil, divided
- ½ cup thinly sliced onion
- ½ cup thinly sliced red bell pepper
- ½ cup thinly sliced green bell pepper
- 1 package (11 ounces) refrigerated French bread dough
- 2 cloves garlic, minced
- ½ teaspoon dried rosemary
- ⅛ teaspoon red pepper flakes (optional)
- ⅓ cup pitted kalamata olives, coarsely chopped
- ¼ cup grated Parmesan cheese

1. Preheat oven to 350°F.

2. Heat 1 tablespoon oil in large skillet over medium-high heat. Add onion and bell peppers; cook and stir 5 minutes or until onion begins to brown. Remove from heat.

3. Unroll dough on nonstick baking sheet. Combine garlic and remaining 1 tablespoon oil in small bowl; spread evenly over dough. Sprinkle with rosemary and red pepper flakes, if desired. Top with onion mixture; sprinkle with olives.

4. Bake 16 to 18 minutes or until golden brown. Sprinkle with Parmesan cheese. Cool on wire rack. Cut flatbread in half lengthwise; cut crosswise into 1-inch-wide strips.

# GREEK STUFFED PEPPERS

**MAKES 4 SERVINGS**

4 medium green bell peppers

1½ cups water, divided

¾ cup cooked quick-cooking brown rice

1 ounce pine nuts, toasted

¾ cup (3 ounces) crumbled reduced-fat feta cheese

12 pitted kalamata olives, chopped

½ cup grape tomatoes, quartered

¼ cup chopped fresh basil

Lemon wedges (optional)

**1.** Slice off tops of bell peppers, about ¼ inch from top, remove and discard stems and seeds. Place peppers in glass 9-inch deep-dish pie pan. Pour ¼ cup water around peppers, cover with plastic wrap and microwave on HIGH 9 to 10 minutes or until tender.

**2.** Meanwhile, bring remaining 1¼ cups water to a boil in medium saucepan over high heat. Add rice, cover and reduce heat; simmer 10 to 12 minutes or until water is absorbed and rice is tender.

**3.** Remove peppers from pan and drain water. Return peppers to pan, cut side up.

**4.** Remove rice from heat, gently stir in remaining ingredients except lemon wedges. Spoon equal amounts of rice mixture into each pepper. Serve with lemon wedges, if desired.

# EGGPLANT PARMESAN

**MAKES 12 SERVINGS**

- 2 eggs
- 1 teaspoon dried basil
- ½ teaspoon salt
- ¼ teaspoon black pepper
- ½ cup plus 2 tablespoons grated Parmesan cheese, divided
- 1 package (3 ounces) ramen noodles, any flavor, crushed*
- ¼ cup panko or other bread crumbs
- 2 medium eggplants (1 pound each), cut lengthwise into ¾-inch slices
-   Vegetable oil
- 1 cup low-fat ricotta cheese
- 8 ounces (2 cups) shredded mozzarella cheese
- 1 can (about 28 ounces) tomato sauce

*Discard seasoning packet.*

1. Preheat oven to 350°F. Spray 13×9-inch baking pan with nonstick cooking spray.

2. Beat eggs, basil, salt and pepper in shallow dish until blended. Combine ½ cup Parmesan cheese, crushed noodles and panko in another shallow dish. Dip eggplant in egg mixture; shake off excess. Coat both sides with crumb mixture.

3. Heat oil in large skillet. Cook eggplant in batches 4 minutes or until golden, turning once. Drain on paper towel-lined plate.

4. Combine ricotta cheese and mozzarella cheese in small bowl. Place one third of eggplant in bottom of prepared pan. Spread about 1 cup tomato sauce over eggplant. Top with half of cheese mixture; repeat layers ending with sauce. Bake 30 minutes or until eggplant is fork-tender and cheese is melted.

5. Preheat broiler. Sprinkle remaining 2 tablespoons Parmesan cheese over eggplant. Broil 6 inches from heat 3 minutes or until cheese is browned. Let stand 10 minutes before serving.

**TIP:** Use one hand to dip the eggplant in the egg mixture and the other hand to coat with crumbs. This way, your hands will not mix up the mixtures and create a larger mess.

# CHICKEN TZATZIKI PITAS

**MAKES 4 SERVINGS**

- ½ cup plain nonfat Greek yogurt
- ¼ cup finely chopped cucumber
- 2 teaspoons lemon juice
- 2 teaspoons chopped fresh mint
- 1 clove garlic, crushed
- ¼ teaspoon salt
- Dash black pepper
- 1 cup chopped cooked chicken
- 1 cup chopped romaine lettuce
- ½ cup chopped tomatoes
- 2 tablespoons chopped red onion
- 2 tablespoons chopped kalamata olives
- 4 (6-inch) whole wheat pita bread halves

**1.** Stir together yogurt, cucumber, lemon juice, mint, garlic, salt and pepper in small bowl; set aside.

**2.** Divide chicken, lettuce, tomatoes, onion and olives evenly among pita halves. Drizzle with sauce.

# GREEK SKILLET LINGUINE

**MAKES 4 SERVINGS**

½ pound uncooked linguine

½ (3-ounce) package dehydrated sun-dried tomatoes

1 cup boiling water

3 tablespoons extra virgin olive oil, divided

½ cup chopped onion

4 cloves garlic, minced

1½ pounds raw large shrimp, peeled and deveined

1¼ teaspoons dried oregano

½ teaspoon salt or to taste

2 cans artichoke hearts, well-drained and cut into quarters

14 kalamata or black olives, pitted and coarsely chopped

2 tablespoons balsamic vinegar

⅓ cup crumbled feta cheese

1. Cook pasta according to package directions; drain.

2. Meanwhile, place sun-dried tomatoes in small bowl. Add 1 cup boiling water; let stand 10 minutes. Drain well and chop.

3. Heat 1 tablespoon oil in large skillet over medium-high heat 1 minute. Add onion and garlic; cook and stir 3 minutes. Add shrimp, oregano and salt; cook 4 to 5 minutes or until shrimp are opaque, stirring frequently. Add artichoke hearts, olives and reserved tomatoes. Stir gently; cook 3 minutes.

4. Remove skillet from heat. Gently stir in vinegar and remaining 2 tablespoons oil. Cover; let stand 5 minutes. Serve shrimp mixture over pasta and sprinkle with feta cheese.

# FALAFEL WITH GARLIC TAHINI SAUCE

MAKES 8 SERVINGS

1 cup dried chickpeas, rinsed and sorted

Garlic Tahini Sauce (recipe follows)

1 small onion, chopped

½ cup chopped fresh parsley

2 cloves garlic

2 teaspoons ground cumin

1 teaspoon ground coriander

½ teaspoon salt

½ teaspoon ground red pepper

1 tablespoon lemon juice

Vegetable oil

Pita bread, lettuce, tomatoes, chopped cucumbers (optional)

1. Soak chickpeas overnight in large bowl with water to cover by at least 3 inches. (Chickpeas will triple in volume.) Prepare Garlic Tahini Sauce; refrigerate until ready to serve.

2. Drain chickpeas well and transfer to food processor. Add all remaining ingredients except oil. Pulse until mixture is smooth, scraping side of bowl frequently. If mixture is too dry, add 1 to 2 tablespoons water.

3. Scoop out heaping tablespoons of mixture. Shape into 1½-inch balls with dampened hands. Place on baking sheet lined with waxed paper.

4. Pour oil into deep heavy saucepan to depth of 2 inches. Heat over medium-high heat to 350°F. Fry falafel in batches 3 to 5 minutes or until golden brown. Remove with slotted spoon and drain on paper towels.

5. Serve with pita bread, lettuce, tomatoes and cucumbers, if desired, accompanied by Garlic Tahini Sauce.

# GARLIC TAHINI SAUCE

MAKES ABOUT 1 CUP

½ cup plain yogurt

¼ cup tahini

3 tablespoons water

2 tablespoons fresh lemon juice

1 clove garlic, minced

½ teaspoon ground cumin

Salt and black pepper to taste

Combine all ingredients in small bowl. Stir with wire whisk until well blended. Cover; refrigerate 1 hour.

# HUMMUS PITA PIZZAS

**MAKES 4 SERVINGS**

- 1 can (about 15 ounces) chickpeas, drained
- 3 tablespoons olive oil
- 2 teaspoons lemon juice
- 1 teaspoon bottled minced garlic
- ¼ teaspoon salt
- ⅛ teaspoon ground red pepper
- 4 pita bread rounds
- 1 cup chopped tomato
- 1 can (4 ounces) sliced black olives, drained
- 1½ cups (6 ounces) shredded mozzarella cheese

1. Preheat oven to 425°F. Combine chickpeas, oil, lemon juice, garlic, salt and red pepper in food processor or blender; process until smooth.

2. Spread bean mixture over pita rounds; top with tomato, olives and cheese. Bake 8 to 10 minutes or until cheese is lightly browned.

**SERVE IT WITH STYLE!:** Add a Cucumber-Yogurt Salad to complete this meal. Just toss chopped seeded cucumbers with plain yogurt. Season with minced garlic, dried dill weed, salt and black pepper to taste.

# SPINACH AND FETA FARRO STUFFED PEPPERS

**MAKES 6 SERVINGS**

- 1 tablespoon olive oil
- 1 package (about 5 ounces) baby spinach
- ½ cup sliced green onions (about 4)
- 2 cloves garlic, crushed
- 1 tablespoon chopped fresh oregano
- 1 package (8.8 ounces) quick-cooking farro, prepared according to package directions using vegetable broth instead of water
- 1 can (about 14 ounces) petite diced tomatoes, drained
- ⅛ teaspoon black pepper
- 1 package (4 ounces) crumbled feta cheese, divided
- 3 large bell peppers, halved lengthwise, cored and ribs removed

1. Preheat oven to 350°F.

2. Heat oil in large skillet over medium-high heat. Add spinach, green onions, garlic and oregano; cook and stir 3 minutes. Stir in farro, tomatoes, black pepper and ½ cup feta cheese.

3. Spoon farro mixture into bell pepper halves (about ¾ cup each); place in shallow baking pan. Pour ¼ cup water into bottom of pan; cover with foil.

4. Bake 30 minutes or until bell peppers are crisp-tender and filling is heated through. Sprinkle with remaining feta cheese.

# CHICKEN, HUMMUS AND VEGETABLE WRAPS

**MAKES 4 SERVINGS**

¾ cup hummus (regular, roasted red pepper or roasted garlic)

4 (8- to 10-inch) sun-dried tomato or spinach wraps *or* whole wheat tortillas

2 cups chopped cooked chicken breast

Chipotle hot pepper sauce or Louisiana-style hot pepper sauce (optional)

½ cup shredded carrots

½ cup chopped unpeeled cucumber

½ cup thinly sliced radishes

2 tablespoons chopped fresh mint *or* basil

Spread hummus evenly over wraps all the way to edges. Arrange chicken over hummus; sprinkle with hot pepper sauce, if desired. Top with carrots, cucumber, radishes and mint. Roll up tightly. Cut in half diagonally.

**VARIATION:** Substitute alfalfa sprouts for the radishes. For tasty appetizers, cut wraps into bite-size pieces.

# LENTIL BOLOGNESE

MAKES 6 TO 8 SERVINGS

2 tablespoons olive oil

1 onion, chopped

1 carrot, chopped

1 stalk celery, chopped

2 cloves garlic, minced

1 teaspoon salt

½ teaspoon dried oregano

Pinch red pepper flakes

3 tablespoons tomato paste

¼ cup dry white wine

1 can (28 ounces) crushed tomatoes

1 can (14 ounces) diced tomatoes

1 cup dried lentils, rinsed

1 portobello mushroom, gills removed, finely chopped

1½ cups water or vegetable broth

Hot cooked pasta

**1.** Heat oil in large saucepan over medium heat. Add onion, carrot and celery; cook and stir 10 minutes or until onion is lightly browned and carrots are softened.

**2.** Stir in garlic, salt, oregano and red pepper flakes. Add tomato paste; cook and stir 1 minute. Add wine; cook and stir until absorbed. Stir in crushed tomatoes, diced tomatoes, lentils, mushroom and water. Bring to a simmer.

**3.** Reduce heat to medium; partially cover and simmer about 40 minutes or until lentils are tender, removing cover after 20 minutes. Serve over pasta.

# GREEK CHICKEN BURGERS WITH CUCUMBER YOGURT SAUCE

MAKES 4 SERVINGS

½ cup plus 2 tablespoons plain nonfat Greek yogurt

½ medium cucumber, peeled, seeded and finely chopped

Juice of ½ lemon

3 cloves garlic, minced, divided

2 teaspoons finely chopped fresh mint *or* ½ teaspoon dried mint

⅛ teaspoon salt

⅛ teaspoon ground white pepper

1 pound ground chicken breast

¾ cup (3 ounces) crumbled reduced-fat feta cheese

4 large kalamata olives, rinsed, patted dry and minced

1 egg

½ to 1 teaspoon dried oregano

¼ teaspoon black pepper

Mixed baby lettuce (optional)

Fresh mint leaves (optional)

1. Combine yogurt, cucumber, lemon juice, 2 cloves garlic, 2 teaspoons chopped mint, salt and white pepper in medium bowl; mix well. Cover and refrigerate until ready to serve.

2. Combine chicken, feta cheese, olives, egg, oregano, black pepper and remaining 1 clove garlic in large bowl; mix well. Shape mixture into four patties.

3. Spray grill pan with nonstick cooking spray; heat over medium-high heat. Grill patties 5 to 7 minutes per side or until cooked through (165°F).

4. Serve burgers with sauce and mixed greens, if desired. Garnish with mint leaves.

# SOUPS & STEWS

## GREEK LEMON AND RICE SOUP

**MAKES 6 TO 8 SERVINGS**

2 tablespoons butter

⅓ cup minced green onions

6 cups chicken broth

⅔ cup uncooked long grain rice

4 eggs

Juice of 1 fresh lemon

⅛ teaspoon white pepper (optional)

Fresh mint and lemon peel (optional)

**1.** Melt butter in medium saucepan over medium heat. Add green onions; cook and stir about 3 minutes or until tender.

**2.** Stir in broth and rice; bring to a boil over medium-high heat. Reduce heat to low; cover and simmer 20 to 25 minutes or until rice is tender.

**3.** Beat eggs in medium bowl. Stir in lemon juice and ½ cup broth mixture until blended. Gradually pour egg mixture into broth mixture in saucepan, stirring constantly. Cook and stir over low heat 2 to 3 minutes or until soup thickens enough to lightly coat spoon. *Do not boil.*

**4.** Stir in pepper, if desired. Garnish with mint and lemon peel, if desired.

# MINESTRONE SOUP

MAKES 4 TO 6 SERVINGS

- 1 tablespoon olive oil
- ½ cup chopped onion
- 1 stalk celery, diced
- 1 carrot, diced
- 2 cloves garlic, minced
- 2 cups vegetable broth
- 1½ cups water
- 1 bay leaf
- ¾ teaspoon salt
- ½ teaspoon dried basil
- ½ teaspoon dried oregano
- ¼ teaspoon dried thyme
- ¼ teaspoon sugar
- Ground black pepper
- 1 can (about 15 ounces) dark red kidney beans, rinsed and drained
- 1 can (about 15 ounces) navy beans or cannellini beans, rinsed and drained
- 1 can (about 14 ounces) diced tomatoes
- 1 cup diced zucchini (about 1 small)
- ½ cup uncooked small shell pasta
- ½ cup frozen cut green beans
- ¼ cup dry red wine
- 1 cup packed chopped fresh spinach
- Grated Parmesan cheese (optional)

**1.** Heat oil in large saucepan or Dutch oven over medium-high heat. Add onion, celery, carrot and garlic; cook and stir 5 to 7 minutes or until vegetables are tender. Add broth, water, bay leaf, salt, basil, oregano, thyme, sugar and pepper; bring to a boil.

**2.** Stir in kidney beans, navy beans, tomatoes, zucchini, pasta, green beans and wine; cook 10 minutes, stirring occasionally.

**3.** Add spinach; cook 2 minutes or until pasta and zucchini are tender. Remove and discard bay leaf. Ladle into bowls; garnish with Parmesan cheese.

# FRESH TOMATO PASTA SOUP

**MAKES 8 SERVINGS**

- 1 tablespoon olive oil
- ½ cup chopped onion
- 1 clove garlic, minced
- 3 pounds fresh tomatoes (about 9 medium), coarsely chopped
- 3 cups fat-free reduced-sodium chicken broth
- 1 tablespoon minced fresh basil
- 1 tablespoon minced fresh marjoram
- 1 tablespoon minced fresh oregano
- 1 teaspoon whole fennel seeds
- ½ teaspoon black pepper
- ¾ cup uncooked rosamarina, orzo or other small pasta
- ½ cup (2 ounces) shredded part-skim mozzarella cheese

1. Heat oil in large saucepan over medium heat. Add onion and garlic; cook and stir until onion is tender.

2. Add tomatoes, broth, basil, marjoram, oregano, fennel seeds and pepper; bring to a boil. Reduce heat to low; cover and simmer 25 minutes. Remove from heat; cool slightly.

3. Purée tomato mixture in batches in food processor or blender. Return to saucepan; bring to a boil. Add pasta; cook 7 to 9 minutes or until tender. Sprinkle with cheese.

# MIDDLE EASTERN BUTTERNUT SQUASH SOUP

**MAKES 6 SERVINGS**

1 medium butternut squash (about 2 pounds)

2 teaspoons olive oil

1 medium onion, chopped

2 carrots, sliced

1 stalk celery, sliced

2 cloves garlic

3 cups fat-free chicken or vegetable broth

1 teaspoon ground cinnamon

1 teaspoon green pepper sauce

¾ teaspoon salt

½ teaspoon ground coriander

6 slices French bread, toasted

Chopped fresh parsley

1. Peel squash. Cut into quarters; remove and discard seeds. Cut squash into cubes; set aside.

2. Heat oil in 3-quart saucepan until hot. Add onion, carrots and celery; cook and stir about 4 minutes. Add garlic; cook and stir 1 minute.

3. Add squash, broth, cinnamon, pepper sauce, salt and coriander to saucepan. Bring broth to a boil over high heat. Cover; reduce heat and simmer 15 minutes or until squash is tender. Remove from heat.

4. Transfer squash mixture to food processor in batches. Process until smooth. Return to saucepan.

5. Ladle soup into bowls. Top with toast and sprinkle with parsley.

**TIP:** An easier way to purée the soup is to use an immersion blender. It's a small appliance that you place into the soup to purée it right in the saucepan. It's faster and less messy.

# LEMON-MINT MEATBALLS WITH LEMON ORZO

**MAKES 4 SERVINGS (3 MEATBALLS EACH)**

- 12 ounces ground chicken
- 2 green onions, minced
- 2 tablespoons minced fresh mint
- 2 tablespoons cholesterol-free egg substitute
- 3 teaspoons grated lemon peel, divided
- 6 cloves garlic, divided
- ½ teaspoon dried oregano
- ¼ teaspoon black pepper
- 3 cups fat-free reduced-sodium chicken broth
- 1 cup (6 ounces) uncooked orzo pasta
- 1 tablespoon lemon juice
- ½ of 10-ounce package fresh spinach leaves, washed and torn

1. Spray 11×7-inch microwavable baking dish with nonstick cooking spray. Combine chicken, green onions, mint, egg substitute, 2 teaspoons lemon peel, 3 minced cloves garlic, oregano and pepper in medium bowl; mix until well blended. Shape into 12 meatballs and place in baking dish, spacing evenly apart.

2. Slice remaining 3 cloves garlic; place in large saucepan. Add chicken broth; bring to a boil over high heat. Stir in orzo. Reduce heat to medium; simmer 8 to 10 minutes or until tender. Reduce heat to low; stir in remaining 1 teaspoon lemon peel and lemon juice. Stir in spinach, one handful at a time, until incorporated. Stir until spinach is wilted. Remove from heat; cover to keep warm.

3. Place meatballs in microwave. Microwave on HIGH 2 minutes. Rearrange meatballs, moving them from outer edges to center of pan. Microwave on HIGH 1 to 2 minutes more until cooked through (160°F).

4. Spoon orzo mixture into wide bowls or rimmed plates. Top with meatballs.

# PASTA FAGIOLI SOUP

**MAKES 5 TO 6 SERVINGS**

2 cans (about 14 ounces each) reduced-sodium beef or vegetable broth

1 can (about 15 ounces) Great Northern beans, rinsed and drained

1 can (about 14 ounces) diced tomatoes

2 zucchini, quartered lengthwise and sliced

1 tablespoon olive oil

1½ teaspoons minced garlic

½ teaspoon dried basil

½ teaspoon dried oregano

½ cup uncooked tubetti, ditalini or small shell pasta

½ cup garlic seasoned croutons

½ cup grated Asiago or Romano cheese

3 tablespoons chopped fresh basil or Italian parsley (optional)

**SLOW COOKER DIRECTIONS**

1. Combine broth, beans, tomatoes, zucchini, oil, garlic, dried basil and oregano in slow cooker; mix well. Cover; cook on LOW 3 to 4 hours.

2. Stir in pasta. Cover; cook on LOW 1 hour or until pasta is tender.

3. Serve soup with croutons and cheese. Garnish with fresh basil.

**TIP:** Only small pasta varieties like tubetti, ditalini or small shell-shaped pasta should be used in this recipe. The low heat of a slow cooker won't allow larger pasta shapes to cook completely.

# MIDDLE EASTERN VEGETABLE STEW

**MAKES 6 SERVINGS**

¼ cup olive oil

3 cups (12 ounces) sliced zucchini

2 cups (6 ounces) cubed peeled eggplant

2 cups sliced quartered peeled sweet potatoes

1½ cups cubed peeled butternut squash (optional)

1 can (28 ounces) crushed tomatoes in purée

1 cup drained canned chickpeas

½ cup raisins or currants (optional)

1½ teaspoons ground cinnamon

1 teaspoon grated orange peel

¾ teaspoon ground cumin

½ teaspoon salt

½ teaspoon paprika

¼ to ½ teaspoon ground red pepper

⅛ teaspoon ground cardamom

Hot cooked whole wheat couscous or brown rice (optional)

**1.** Heat oil in Dutch oven or large saucepan over medium heat. Add zucchini, eggplant, sweet potatoes and squash, if desired; cook and stir 8 to 10 minutes until vegetables are slightly softened. Stir in tomatoes, chickpeas, raisins, if desired, cinnamon, orange peel, cumin, salt, paprika, red pepper and cardamom; bring to a boil over high heat.

**2.** Reduce heat to low; cover and simmer 30 minutes or until vegetables are tender. If sauce becomes too thick, stir in water to thin. Serve over couscous, if desired.

# CHICKPEA-VEGETABLE SOUP

MAKES 4 SERVINGS

1 teaspoon olive oil

1 cup chopped onion

½ cup chopped green bell pepper

2 cloves garlic, minced

2 cans (about 14 ounces each) no-salt-added chopped tomatoes

3 cups water

2 cups broccoli florets

1 can (about 15 ounces) chickpeas, rinsed, drained and slightly mashed

½ cup (3 ounces) uncooked orzo or rosamarina pasta

1 whole bay leaf

1 tablespoon chopped fresh thyme *or* 1 teaspoon dried thyme

1 tablespoon chopped fresh rosemary leaves *or* 1 teaspoon dried rosemary

1 tablespoon lime or lemon juice

½ teaspoon ground turmeric

¼ teaspoon salt

¼ teaspoon ground red pepper

¼ cup pumpkin seeds or sunflower kernels

**1.** Heat oil in large saucepan over medium heat. Add onion, bell pepper and garlic; cook and stir 5 minutes or until vegetables are tender.

**2.** Add tomatoes, water, broccoli, chickpeas, orzo, bay leaf, thyme, rosemary, lime juice, turmeric, salt and red pepper. Bring to a boil over high heat. Reduce heat to medium-low; cover and simmer 10 to 12 minutes or until orzo is tender.

**3.** Remove and discard bay leaf. Ladle soup into four serving bowls; sprinkle with pumpkin seeds.

# ITALIAN WEDDING SOUP

MAKES 8 SERVINGS

## MEATBALLS

- 2 eggs
- 6 cloves garlic, minced, divided
- 1 teaspoon salt
- ⅛ teaspoon black pepper
- 1½ pounds meatloaf mix (ground beef and pork)
- ¾ cup plain dry bread crumbs
- ½ cup grated Parmesan cheese

## SOUP

- 2 tablespoons olive oil
- 1 onion, chopped
- 2 carrots, chopped
- 4 cloves garlic, minced
- 2 heads escarole or curly endive, coarsely chopped
- 8 cups chicken broth
- 1 can (about 14 ounces) Italian plum tomatoes, undrained, coarsely chopped
- 3 sprigs fresh thyme
- 1 teaspoon salt
- ½ teaspoon red pepper flakes
- 1 cup uncooked acini di pepe pasta

1. Whisk eggs, 2 cloves garlic, 1 teaspoon salt and black pepper in large bowl until blended. Stir in meatloaf mix, bread crumbs and Parmesan cheese; mix gently until well blended. Shape mixture by tablespoonfuls into 1-inch balls.

2. Heat oil in large saucepan or Dutch oven over medium heat. Cook meatballs in batches 5 minutes or until browned. Remove to plate; set aside.

3. Add onion, carrots and 4 cloves garlic to saucepan; cook and stir 5 minutes or until onion is lightly browned. Add escarole; cook 2 minutes or until wilted. Stir in broth, tomatoes with juice, thyme, 1 teaspoon salt and red pepper flakes; bring to a boil over high heat. Reduce heat to medium-low; cook 15 minutes.

4. Add meatballs and pasta to soup; return to a boil over high heat. Reduce heat to medium; cook 10 minutes or until pasta is tender. Remove and discard thyme sprigs before serving.

# MEDITERRANEAN EGGPLANT AND WHITE BEAN STEW

MAKES 6 SERVINGS

- 1 tablespoon olive oil
- 1 medium onion, chopped
- 1 medium eggplant (1 pound), peeled and cut into ¾-inch chunks
- 4 cloves garlic, minced
- 1 can (28 ounces) stewed tomatoes, undrained
- 2 bell peppers (1 red and 1 yellow), cut into ¾-inch chunks
- 1 teaspoon dried oregano
- ¼ teaspoon red pepper flakes (optional)
- 1 can (about 15 ounces) Great Northern or cannellini beans, rinsed and drained
- 6 tablespoons grated Parmesan cheese
- ¼ cup chopped fresh basil

1. Heat oil in large saucepan over medium heat. Add onion; cook and stir 5 minutes. Add eggplant and garlic; cook and stir 5 minutes. Stir in tomatoes with juice, bell peppers, oregano and red pepper flakes, if desired. Reduce heat to medium-low; cover and simmer 20 minutes or until vegetables are tender.

2. Stir in beans; simmer uncovered 5 minutes. Ladle into shallow bowls; top with Parmesan cheese and basil.

# FASOLADA (GREEK WHITE BEAN SOUP)

**MAKES 4 TO 6 SERVINGS**

- 4 tablespoons olive oil, divided
- 1 large onion, diced
- 3 stalks celery, diced
- 3 carrots, diced
- 4 cloves garlic, minced
- ¼ cup tomato paste
- 1 teaspoon salt
- 1 teaspoon dried oregano
- ½ teaspoon ground cumin
- ¼ teaspoon black pepper
- 1 bay leaf
- 1 container (32 ounces) vegetable broth
- 3 cans (15 ounces each) cannellini beans, rinsed and drained
- 2 tablespoons lemon juice
- ¼ cup minced fresh parsley

**1.** Heat 2 tablespoons oil in large saucepan over medium-high heat. Add onion, celery and carrots; cook and stir 8 to 10 minutes or until vegetables are softened. Stir in garlic; cook and stir 30 seconds. Stir in tomato paste, salt, oregano, cumin, black pepper and bay leaf; cook and stir 30 seconds.

**2.** Stir in broth; bring to a boil. Stir in beans; return to a boil. Reduce heat to medium-low; simmer 30 minutes. Stir in remaining 2 tablespoons oil and lemon juice. Remove and discard bay leaf. Sprinkle with parsley just before serving.

# MIDDLE EASTERN LENTIL SOUP

**MAKES 4 SERVINGS**

1 cup dried lentils

2 tablespoons olive oil

1 small onion, chopped

1 medium red bell pepper, chopped

1 teaspoon whole fennel seeds

½ teaspoon ground cumin

¼ teaspoon ground red pepper

4 cups water

½ teaspoon salt

1 tablespoon lemon juice

½ cup plain low-fat yogurt

2 tablespoons chopped fresh parsley

1. Rinse lentils, discarding any debris or blemished lentils; drain.

2. Heat oil in large saucepan over medium-high heat until hot. Add onion and bell pepper; cook and stir 5 minutes or until tender. Add fennel seeds, cumin and ground red pepper; cook and stir 1 minute.

3. Add water, lentils and salt. Bring to a boil. Reduce heat to low. Cover and simmer 25 to 30 minutes or until lentils are tender. Stir in lemon juice.

4. To serve, ladle soup into individual bowls and top with yogurt; sprinkle with parsley.

**TIP:** Serve with homemade pita chips. Cut 4 pita bread rounds into 6 wedges each. Toss wedges with 1 tablespoon olive oil and 1 teaspoon coarse salt; spread on large baking sheet. Bake at 350°F 15 minutes or until light brown and crisp.

# MEDITERRANEAN CHILI

**MAKES 5 SERVINGS**

- 1 tablespoon olive oil
- ½ cup chopped onion
- 2 bell peppers, coarsely chopped (1 green and 1 yellow)
- 4 cloves garlic, minced
- 1 can (about 15 ounces) no-salt-added chickpeas, drained
- 1 can (about 14 ounces) no-salt-added stewed tomatoes, undrained
- 1 cup low-sodium vegetable juice
- ¼ teaspoon crushed red pepper flakes
- ½ cup (2 ounces) crumbled reduced-fat feta cheese
- ¼ cup chopped fresh basil

1. Heat oil in large saucepan over medium heat. Add onion; cook 5 minutes, stirring occasionally. Add bell peppers and garlic; cook 5 minutes, stirring occasionally.

2. Stir in chickpeas, tomatoes with juice, vegetable juice and red pepper flakes; bring to a boil over high heat. Reduce heat to low; simmer, uncovered, 12 minutes or until vegetables are tender.

3. Ladle into shallow bowls; top with feta cheese and basil.

# SPICY AFRICAN CHICKPEA AND SWEET POTATO STEW

**MAKES 4 SERVINGS**

Spice Paste (recipe follows)

1½ pounds sweet potatoes, peeled and cubed

2 cups vegetable broth or water

1 can (about 15 ounces) chickpeas, rinsed and drained

1 can (about 14 ounces) plum tomatoes, undrained, chopped

1½ cups sliced fresh okra *or* 1 package (10 ounces) frozen cut okra, thawed

Yellow Couscous (recipe follows)

Hot pepper sauce

Fresh cilantro (optional)

1. Prepare Spice Paste.

2. Combine sweet potatoes, broth, chickpeas, tomatoes with juice, okra and Spice Paste in large saucepan. Bring to a boil over high heat. Reduce heat to low. Cover and simmer 15 minutes. Uncover; simmer 10 minutes or until vegetables are tender.

3. Meanwhile, prepare Yellow Couscous.

4. Serve stew with Yellow Couscous and hot pepper sauce. Garnish with cilantro.

# SPICE PASTE

6 cloves garlic, peeled

1 teaspoon coarse salt

2 teaspoons paprika

1½ teaspoons whole cumin seeds

1 teaspoon black pepper

½ teaspoon ground ginger

½ teaspoon ground allspice

1 tablespoon olive oil

Process garlic and salt in blender or small food processor until garlic is finely chopped. Add remaining seasonings. Process 15 seconds. With blender running, pour in oil through cover opening; blend until mixture forms paste.

# YELLOW COUSCOUS

**MAKES 3 CUPS**

- 1 tablespoon olive oil
- 5 green onions, sliced
- 1⅔ cups water
- ¼ teaspoon salt
- ⅛ teaspoon saffron threads *or* ½ teaspoon ground turmeric
- 1 cup uncooked couscous

Heat oil in medium saucepan over medium heat. Add green onions; cook and stir 4 minutes. Add water, salt and saffron. Bring to a boil; stir in couscous. Remove from heat. Cover; let stand 5 minutes.

# CHICKEN & TURKEY

## FORTY-CLOVE CHICKEN FILICE

MAKES 4 TO 6 SERVINGS

¼ cup olive oil

1 cut-up whole chicken (about 3 pounds)

40 cloves garlic (about 2 heads), peeled

4 stalks celery, thickly sliced

½ cup dry white wine

¼ cup dry vermouth

Grated peel and juice of 1 lemon

2 tablespoons finely chopped fresh parsley

2 teaspoons dried basil

1 teaspoon dried oregano, crushed

Pinch red pepper flakes

Salt and black pepper

1. Preheat oven to 375°F.

2. Heat oil in Dutch oven. Add chicken; cook until browned on all sides.

3. Combine garlic, celery, wine, vermouth, lemon juice, parsley, basil, oregano and red pepper flakes in medium bowl; pour over chicken. Sprinkle with lemon peel; season with salt and black pepper.

4. Cover and bake 40 minutes. Remove cover; bake 15 minutes or until chicken is cooked through (165°F).

# SPICED CHICKEN SKEWERS WITH YOGURT-TAHINI SAUCE

MAKES 8 SERVINGS

1 cup plain nonfat or regular Greek yogurt

¼ cup chopped fresh parsley, plus additional for garnish

¼ cup tahini

2 tablespoons lemon juice

1 clove garlic

¾ teaspoon salt, divided

1 tablespoon vegetable oil

2 teaspoons garam masala

1 pound boneless skinless chicken breasts, cut into 1-inch pieces

1. Spray grill grid with nonstick cooking spray. Prepare grill for direct cooking.

2. For sauce, combine yogurt, ¼ cup parsley, tahini, lemon juice, garlic and ¼ teaspoon salt in food processor or blender; process until smooth. Set aside.

3. Combine oil, garam masala and remaining ½ teaspoon salt in medium bowl. Add chicken; toss to coat. Thread chicken on eight 6-inch wooden or metal skewers.*

4. Grill chicken skewers over medium-high heat 5 minutes per side or until chicken is no longer pink. Serve with sauce. Garnish with additional parsley.

*If using wooden skewers, soak in cold water 20 to 30 minutes to prevent burning.

# ROAST CHICKEN & POTATOES CATALAN

MAKES 4 SERVINGS

2 tablespoons olive oil

2 tablespoons lemon juice

1 teaspoon dried thyme

½ teaspoon salt

¼ teaspoon ground red pepper

¼ teaspoon ground saffron *or* ½ teaspoon crushed saffron threads or turmeric

2 large baking potatoes (about 1½ pounds), cut into 1½-inch pieces

4 skinless bone-in chicken breasts (about 2 pounds)

1 cup sliced red bell pepper

1 cup frozen peas, thawed

Lemon wedges (optional)

1. Preheat oven to 400°F. Spray large shallow roasting pan or 15×10-inch jelly-roll pan with nonstick cooking spray.

2. Combine oil, lemon juice, thyme, salt, ground red pepper and saffron in large bowl; mix well. Add potatoes; toss to coat.

3. Arrange potatoes in single layer around edges of pan. Place chicken in center of pan; brush both sides of chicken with remaining oil mixture in bowl.

4. Bake 20 minutes. Turn potatoes; baste chicken with pan juices. Add bell pepper; continue baking 20 minutes or until chicken is no longer pink in center, juices run clear and potatoes are browned. Stir peas into potato mixture; bake 5 minutes or until heated through. Garnish with lemon wedges.

# GREEK CHICKEN & SPINACH RICE CASSEROLE

MAKES 4 SERVINGS

1 cup finely chopped onion

1 package (10 ounces) frozen chopped spinach, thawed and squeezed dry

1 cup uncooked quick-cooking brown rice

1 cup water

¼ teaspoon salt

⅛ teaspoon ground red pepper

¾ pound chicken tenders

2 teaspoons Greek seasoning (oregano, rosemary and sage mixture)

½ teaspoon salt-free lemon-pepper seasoning

1 tablespoon olive oil

1 lemon, cut into wedges

1. Preheat oven to 350°F. Spray large ovenproof skillet with nonstick cooking spray; heat over medium heat. Add onion; cook and stir 2 minutes or until translucent. Add spinach, rice, water, salt and red pepper. Stir until well blended. Remove from heat.

2. Place chicken on top of mixture in skillet in single layer. Sprinkle with Greek seasoning and lemon-pepper seasoning. Cover with foil. Bake 25 minutes or until chicken is no longer pink in center.

3. Remove foil. Drizzle oil evenly over top. Serve with lemon wedges.

# TURKEY MEATBALLS WITH YOGURT-CUCUMBER SAUCE

MAKES 40 MEATBALLS

2 tablespoons olive oil, divided

1 cup finely chopped onion

2 cloves garlic, minced

1¼ pounds lean ground turkey or ground lamb

½ cup plain dry bread crumbs

¼ cup whipping cream

1 egg, lightly beaten

3 tablespoons chopped fresh mint

1 teaspoon salt

⅛ teaspoon ground red pepper

Yogurt-Cucumber Sauce (recipe follows)

1. Line two baking sheets with parchment paper. Heat 1 tablespoon oil in medium skillet over medium-high heat. Add onion; cook and stir 3 minutes or until softened. Add garlic; cook and stir 30 seconds. Let cool slightly.

2. Combine turkey, onion mixture, bread crumbs, cream, egg, mint, salt and red pepper in large bowl; mix well. Shape into 40 meatballs. Place meatballs on prepared baking sheets. Cover with plastic wrap; refrigerate 1 hour.

3. Meanwhile, prepare Yogurt-Cucumber Sauce. Preheat oven to 400°F. Brush meatballs with remaining 1 tablespoon oil. Bake 15 to 20 minutes or until cooked through, turning once during baking. Serve with Yogurt-Cucumber Sauce.

# YOGURT-CUCUMBER SAUCE

MAKES ABOUT 1 CUP

1 container (6 ounces) plain nonfat Greek yogurt

½ cup peeled seeded and finely chopped cucumber

2 teaspoons chopped fresh mint

2 teaspoons grated lemon peel

2 teaspoons lemon juice

¼ teaspoon salt

Combine all ingredients in small bowl. Refrigerate until ready to serve.

# PROVENÇAL LEMON AND OLIVE CHICKEN

MAKES 8 SERVINGS

- 2 cups chopped onions
- 8 skinless chicken thighs (about 2½ pounds)
- 1 lemon, thinly sliced and seeded
- 1 cup pitted green olives
- 1 tablespoon olive brine or white vinegar
- 2 teaspoons herbes de Provence
- 1 bay leaf
- ½ teaspoon salt
- ⅛ teaspoon black pepper
- 1 cup chicken broth
- ½ cup minced fresh Italian parsley
  Hot cooked rice

SLOW COOKER DIRECTIONS

1. Place onions in slow cooker. Arrange chicken thighs and lemon slices over onion. Add olives, brine, herbes de Provence, bay leaf, salt and pepper. Pour in broth.

2. Cover; cook on LOW 5 to 6 hours or on HIGH 3 to 3½ hours or until chicken is tender. Remove and discard bay leaf. Stir in parsley before serving. Serve over rice.

NOTE: To skin chicken thighs easily, grasp skin with paper towel and pull away. Repeat with fresh paper towel for each piece of chicken, discarding skins and towels.

# BROILED TURKEY TENDERLOIN KABOBS

MAKES 4 SERVINGS

¼ cup orange juice

2 tablespoons reduced-sodium soy sauce, divided

1 clove garlic, minced

1 teaspoon fresh grated ginger

12 ounces turkey tenderloins (about 2 medium), cut into 1-inch cubes

1 tablespoon molasses

1 green bell pepper, cut into 1-inch pieces

1 red onion, cut into 1½-inch pieces

1 cup hot cooked brown rice

1. Combine orange juice, 1 tablespoon soy sauce, garlic and ginger in large bowl; stir to blend. Remove half of mixture; cover and refrigerate. Add turkey to remaining mixture. Cover; marinate 2 hours, stirring occasionally.

2. Line large baking sheet with foil; spray with nonstick cooking spray. Remove turkey from marinade; discard marinade. Add remaining 1 tablespoon soy sauce and molasses to reserved half of marinade; whisk until smooth and well blended.

3. Set oven to broil. Alternately thread turkey, bell pepper and onion on four skewers.* Place on prepared baking sheet.

4. Broil 4 inches from heat source 3 minutes. Brush evenly with reserved marinade mixture. Broil 6 to 9 minutes or until turkey is no longer pink.

5. Spoon ¼ cup brown rice onto four plates. Top each with 1 skewer.

*If using wooden skewers, soak in cold water 20 to 30 minutes to prevent burning.

# GREEK CHICKEN AND ORZO

MAKES 8 SERVINGS

2 medium green bell peppers, cut into thin strips

1 cup chopped onion

2 teaspoons extra virgin olive oil

8 skinless chicken thighs, rinsed and patted dry

1 tablespoon dried oregano

½ teaspoon dried rosemary

½ teaspoon garlic powder

¾ teaspoon salt, divided

⅜ teaspoon black pepper, divided

8 ounces uncooked dry orzo pasta

Juice and grated peel of 1 medium lemon

½ cup water

½ cup (2 ounces) crumbled feta cheese (optional)

Chopped fresh parsley (optional)

## SLOW COOKER DIRECTIONS

1. Coat 6-quart slow cooker with nonstick cooking spray. Add bell peppers and onion.

2. Heat oil in large skillet over medium-high heat until hot. Brown chicken on both sides. Transfer to slow cooker, overlapping slightly if necessary. Sprinkle chicken with oregano, rosemary, garlic powder, ¼ teaspoon salt and ⅛ teaspoon black pepper. Cover; cook on LOW 5 to 6 hours or on HIGH 3 hours.

3. Transfer chicken to separate plate. Turn slow cooker to HIGH. Stir orzo, lemon juice, lemon peel, water and remaining ½ teaspoon salt and ¼ teaspoon black pepper into slow cooker. Top with chicken. Cover; cook on HIGH 30 minutes or until pasta is done. Garnish with feta cheese and parsley, if desired.

NOTE: To skin chicken easily, grasp skin with paper towel and pull away. Repeat with fresh paper towel for each piece of chicken, discarding skins and towels.

# GREEK-STYLE CHICKEN STEW

MAKES 6 SERVINGS

3 pounds skinless chicken breasts

All-purpose flour

2 cups cubed peeled eggplant

2 cups sliced mushrooms

¾ cup coarsely chopped onion (about 1 medium)

2 cloves garlic, minced

1 teaspoon dried oregano

½ teaspoon dried basil

½ teaspoon dried thyme

2 cups fat-free reduced-sodium chicken broth

¼ cup dry sherry or additional fat-free reduced-sodium chicken broth

¼ teaspoon salt

¼ teaspoon black pepper

1 can (14 ounces) artichoke hearts, drained

3 cups hot cooked wide egg noodles

1. Coat chicken very lightly with flour. Generously coat nonstick Dutch oven or large nonstick skillet with nonstick cooking spray; heat over medium heat. Add chicken; cook 10 to 15 minutes or until browned on all sides. Remove chicken; drain fat from Dutch oven.

2. Add eggplant, mushrooms, onion, garlic, oregano, basil and thyme to Dutch oven; cook and stir over medium heat 5 minutes.

3. Return chicken to Dutch oven. Stir in broth, sherry, salt and pepper; bring to a boil. Reduce heat to low; simmer, covered, 1 hour or until chicken is cooked through. Add artichoke hearts during last 20 minutes of cooking. Serve over noodles. Garnish as desired.

# CHICKEN CACCIATORE

MAKES 4 TO 6 SERVINGS

1 tablespoon olive oil

1 broiler-fryer chicken
  (3 to 3½ pounds), cut into
  8 pieces

4 ounces mushrooms, finely
  chopped

1 medium onion, chopped

1 clove garlic, minced

½ cup dry white wine

1 tablespoon plus
  1½ teaspoons white wine
  vinegar

½ cup chicken broth

1 teaspoon dried basil

½ teaspoon dried marjoram

½ teaspoon salt

⅛ teaspoon black pepper

1 can (about 14 ounces)
  whole tomatoes,
  undrained

8 Italian- or Greek-style
  pitted black olives,
  halved

1 tablespoon chopped fresh
  parsley

  Hot cooked pasta

1. Heat oil in large skillet over medium heat. Add as many chicken pieces in single layer without crowding. Cook 8 minutes per side or until chicken is brown; remove chicken with slotted spatula to Dutch oven. Repeat with remaining chicken pieces.

2. Add mushrooms and onion to drippings in skillet. Cook and stir over medium heat 5 minutes or until onion is soft. Add garlic; cook and stir 30 seconds. Add wine and vinegar; cook over medium-high heat 5 minutes or until liquid is almost evaporated. Stir in broth, basil, marjoram, salt and pepper. Remove from heat.

3. Press tomatoes with juice through sieve into onion mixture; discard seeds. Bring to a boil over medium-high heat; boil, uncovered, 2 minutes. Pour tomato-onion mixture over chicken. Bring to a boil; reduce heat to low. Cover and simmer 25 minutes or until chicken is tender and juices run clear when pierced with fork. Remove chicken with slotted spatula to heated serving dish; keep warm.

4. Bring tomato-onion sauce to a boil over medium-high heat; boil, uncovered, 5 minutes. Add olives and parsley; cook 1 minute. Pour sauce over chicken and pasta.

# MOROCCAN CHICKEN, APRICOT & ALMOND CASSEROLE

MAKES 4 TO 6 SERVINGS

1 pound ground chicken*

¾ teaspoon salt, divided

¼ teaspoon ground cinnamon

¼ teaspoon black pepper

1 tablespoon olive oil

1 small onion, chopped

1 cup sliced dried apricots

1 can (28 ounces) diced tomatoes

½ teaspoon red pepper flakes

½ teaspoon ground ginger

1 can (10½ ounces) condensed chicken broth

½ cup water

1 cup large-pearl couscous**

¼ cup sliced almonds, toasted

*Ground turkey or lamb can be substituted for the ground chicken.

**Large-pearl couscous, which is the size of barley, is available in many supermarkets. If it is not available, substitute regular small-grain couscous.

1. Preheat oven to 325°F.

2. Combine chicken, ½ teaspoon salt, cinnamon and black pepper in medium bowl. Shape into 1-inch balls. Heat oil in large skillet. Add meatballs; brown on all sides. Remove to plate. Add onion and apricots to skillet. Cook 5 minutes over medium heat or until onion is tender. Stir in tomatoes, remaining ¼ teaspoon salt, red pepper flakes and ginger. Simmer 5 minutes.

3. Meanwhile, bring broth and water to a boil in small saucepan. Stir in large-pearl couscous.*** Reduce heat. Cover; simmer 10 minutes or until couscous is tender and almost all liquid has been absorbed. Drain if necessary.

4. Spoon couscous into greased 11×7-inch casserole dish. Top with meatballs; spoon tomato mixture over meatballs. Bake 20 minutes or until chicken is cooked through. Sprinkle with almonds.

***To cook small-grain couscous, follow package directions using 1 cup chicken broth in place of water. Remove from heat and let stand 5 minutes or until all liquid is absorbed. Fluff with a fork.

# MEDITERRANEAN CHICKEN KABOBS OVER COUSCOUS

MAKES 8 SERVINGS

2 pounds boneless skinless chicken breasts *or* chicken tenders, cut into 1-inch pieces

1 small eggplant, peeled and cut into 1-inch pieces

1 medium zucchini, cut crosswise into ½-inch slices

2 medium onions, each cut into 8 wedges

16 medium mushrooms, stemmed

16 cherry tomatoes

1 cup fat-free reduced-sodium chicken broth

⅔ cup balsamic vinegar

3 tablespoons olive oil

2 tablespoons dried mint

4 teaspoons dried basil

1 tablespoon dried oregano

2 teaspoons grated lemon peel

Chopped fresh parsley

4 cups hot cooked couscous

1. Alternately thread chicken, eggplant, zucchini, onions, mushrooms and tomatoes onto 16 metal skewers; place in large glass baking dish.

2. Combine broth, vinegar, oil, mint, basil and oregano in small bowl; pour over kabobs. Cover; marinate in refrigerator 2 hours, turning occasionally. Remove kabobs from marinade; discard marinade.

3. Preheat broiler. Broil kabobs 6 inches from heat 10 to 15 minutes or until chicken is cooked through, turning kabobs halfway through cooking time.

4. Stir lemon peel and parsley into couscous; serve with kabobs.

TIP: These kabobs can be grilled instead of broiled. Spray the grill grid with nonstick cooking spray, then prepare the grill for direct cooking. Grill the kabobs, covered, over medium-hot coals 10 to 15 minutes or until the chicken is cooked through. Turn the kabobs halfway through the cooking time.

# LAMB & MORE

## TUSCAN LAMB SKILLET

**MAKES 4 SERVINGS**

8 lamb rib chops
   (1½ pounds), cut 1 inch
   thick

2 teaspoons olive oil

3 teaspoons minced garlic

1 can (19 ounces) cannellini
   beans, rinsed and
   drained

1 can (about 14 ounces)
   Italian-style tomatoes,
   undrained, coarsely
   chopped

1 tablespoon balsamic
   vinegar

2 teaspoons minced fresh
   rosemary

   Additional fresh rosemary
   (optional)

**1.** Trim fat from lamb chops. Heat oil in large skillet over medium heat. Add lamb; cook about 4 minutes per side or until 160°F for medium doneness. Remove to plate; keep warm.

**2.** Stir garlic into drippings in skillet; cook and stir 1 minute. Stir in beans, tomatoes with juice, vinegar and minced rosemary; bring to a boil. Reduce heat to medium-low; simmer 5 minutes.

**3.** Divide bean mixture among four plates; top with lamb. Garnish with additional rosemary.

# GREEK LAMB BURGERS

**MAKES 4 SERVINGS**

- ¼ cup pine nuts
- 1 pound ground lamb
- ¼ cup finely chopped yellow onion
- 3 cloves garlic, minced, divided
- ¾ teaspoon salt
- ¼ teaspoon black pepper
- ¼ cup plain yogurt
- ¼ teaspoon sugar
- 4 slices red onion (¼ inch thick)
- 1 tablespoon olive oil
- 8 pumpernickel bread slices
- 4 tomato slices
- 12 thin cucumber slices

1. Spread pine nuts in small skillet. Cook over medium heat 1 to 2 minutes or until nuts are lightly browned, stirring frequently.

2. Oil grill grid. Prepare grill for direct cooking. Combine lamb, pine nuts, yellow onion, 2 cloves garlic, salt and pepper in large bowl; mix well. Shape mixture into four patties about ½ inch thick and 4 inches in diameter. Combine yogurt, sugar and remaining 1 clove garlic in small bowl; mix well.

3. Brush one side of each patty and red onion slice with oil; place on grid, oiled sides down. Brush tops with oil. Grill over medium-high heat, covered, 8 to 10 minutes to medium (160°F) or to desired doneness, turning halfway through grilling time. Grill bread 1 to 2 minutes per side during last few minutes of grilling.

4. Serve patties on bread with red onion, tomato, cucumber and yogurt mixture.

# MEDITERRANEAN MEATBALL RATATOUILLE

**MAKES 6 SERVINGS**

- 1 pound bulk mild Italian sausage
- 1 package (8 ounces) sliced mushrooms
- 1 small eggplant, diced
- 1 zucchini, diced
- ½ cup chopped onion
- 1 clove garlic, minced
- 1 teaspoon dried oregano
- 1 teaspoon salt
- ½ teaspoon black pepper
- 2 tomatoes, diced
- 1 tablespoon tomato paste
- 2 tablespoons chopped fresh basil
- 1 teaspoon fresh lemon juice

**SLOW COOKER DIRECTIONS**

**1.** Shape sausage into 1-inch meatballs. Brown meatballs in large skillet over medium heat. Place half the meatballs in 5-quart slow cooker. Add half each of mushrooms, eggplant and zucchini. Top with onion, garlic, ½ teaspoon oregano, ½ teaspoon salt and ¼ teaspoon pepper.

**2.** Add remaining meatballs, mushrooms, eggplant and zucchini, ½ teaspoon oregano, ½ teaspoon salt and ¼ teaspoon pepper. Cover; cook on LOW 6 to 7 hours.

**3.** Stir in diced tomatoes and tomato paste. Cover; cook on LOW 15 minutes. Stir in basil and lemon juice just before serving.

# OPEN-FACED LAMB NAAN SANDWICHES WITH RAITA

MAKES 4 SERVINGS

- 1 tablespoon olive oil
- 1 red onion, diced
- 1 pound ground lamb
- 1¼ teaspoons minced garlic, divided
- 1 tablespoon tomato paste
- 1 teaspoon ground cumin
- ½ teaspoon ground corinader
- 1¾ teaspoons kosher salt, divided
- ¼ cup diced English cucumber
- ¾ cup (6 ounces) plain nonfat Greek yogurt
- 2 tablespoons chopped fresh cilantro
- 4 pieces naan bread, lightly toasted

1. Heat oil in large skillet over medium heat. Add onion; cook about 8 to 10 minutes or until softened. Transfer to small bowl.

2. Cook lamb in same skillet over medium-high heat about 8 minutes or until browned, stirring occasionally. Add 1 teaspoon garlic, tomato paste, cumin, coriander and 1 teaspoon salt; cook 1 minute, stirring constantly. Add onion; cook 1 minute.

3. Combine cucumber, yogurt, remaining ¼ teaspoon garlic, cilantro and remaining ¾ teaspoon salt in medium bowl.

4. Divide lamb evenly among warmed naan; top with raita. Serve immediately.

# MEDITERRANEAN BEEF SKILLET

**MAKES 4 SERVINGS**

2½ cups (about 8 ounces) uncooked whole wheat rotini pasta

1 pound ground beef

½ teaspoon dried basil

½ teaspoon black pepper

1 can (about 14 ounces) diced tomatoes with garlic and onion

1 can (8 ounces) tomato sauce

1 package (about 7 ounces) baby spinach, coarsely chopped

1 can (about 2 ounces) sliced black olives, drained

½ cup (2 ounces) crumbled herb-flavored feta cheese

1. Prepare pasta according to package directions; drain. Cover and keep warm.

2. Brown beef in large skillet over medium-high heat 6 to 8 minutes, stirring to break up meat. Drain fat. Stir in basil and pepper.

3. Reduce heat to medium. Add tomatoes, tomato sauce, spinach and olives; mix well. Cook 10 minutes. Stir in pasta; cook 5 minutes or until heated through. Sprinkle with feta cheese.

# GREEK-STYLE BRAISED LAMB CHOPS

**MAKES 4 SERVINGS**

1 teaspoon Greek seasoning

4 lamb shoulder chops (about 2½ pounds)

3 tablespoons olive oil

1 large onion, halved and sliced

1 bottle (12 ounces) beer

3 plum tomatoes, each cut into 6 wedges

½ cup pitted kalamata olives

1 tablespoon chopped fresh parsley

1. Rub Greek seasoning onto chops.

2. Heat oil in large skillet over medium-high heat. Working in two batches, add chops and brown on all sides. Remove chops to large plate. Add onion to skillet; cook and stir 3 to 5 minutes or until softened. Pour in beer. Bring to a boil over high heat, scraping bottom to loosen browned bits. Reduce heat to low; add chops, tomatoes and olives. Cover and simmer over low heat 1 hour or until meat is tender.

3. Remove chops to serving platter. Remove vegetables to platter using slotted spoon. Tent with foil to keep warm. Bring remaining liquid to a boil over high heat; cook until slightly thickened. Reduce to about 1 cup. Pour sauce over chops and vegetables; sprinkle with parsley.

# FISH & SEAFOOD

## TUNA SICILIAN STYLE

**MAKES 4 SERVINGS**

¾ cup extra virgin olive oil

Juice of 2 lemons

4 cloves garlic, minced

1 tablespoon chopped fresh rosemary *or* 1½ teaspoons dried rosemary

1 tablespoon chopped fresh parsley

¾ teaspoon salt

½ teaspoon black pepper

4 fresh tuna steaks (½ inch thick)

Lemon slices (optional)

Arugula or spinach

**1.** For basting sauce, combine oil, lemon juice, garlic, rosemary, parsley, salt and pepper in small bowl. Prepare grill for direct cooking.*

**2.** Set aside half of basting sauce until ready to serve. Brush both sides of tuna with basting sauce; place on grid over medium-high heat. Grill tuna 4 minutes, basting generously with sauce. Turn and grill 4 to 6 minutes, or until desired degree of doneness, brushing frequently with sauce. Add lemon slices to grill for last few minutes, if desired.

**3.** Transfer tuna to serving dish lined with arugula or spinach and keep warm. Heat reserved sauce in small saucepan over low heat. Drizzle over fish and greens when ready to serve. Garnish with lemon slices.

*Tuna may also be prepared on stovetop grill pan.*

# SHRIMP SCAMPI

MAKES 4 TO 6 SERVINGS

⅓ cup clarified butter*

2 to 4 tablespoons minced garlic

1½ pounds large raw shrimp, peeled and deveined (with tails on)

6 green onions, thinly sliced

¼ cup dry white wine

2 tablespoons lemon juice

Chopped fresh Italian parsley

Salt and black pepper

Lemon wedges (optional)

*To clarify butter, melt butter in small saucepan over low heat. Skim off white foam that forms on top, then strain remaining butter through cheesecloth. Discard cheesecloth and milky residue in bottom of pan. Clarified butter can be stored in airtight container in refrigerator up to 2 months.*

1. Heat butter in large skillet over medium heat. Add garlic; cook and stir 1 to 2 minutes or until softened but not brown. Add shrimp, green onions, wine and lemon juice; cook 2 to 4 minutes or until shrimp are pink and opaque, stirring occasionally.

2. Sprinkle with parsley; season with salt and pepper. Serve with lemon wedges, if desired.

# LEMON-GARLIC SALMON WITH TZATZIKI SAUCE

MAKES 4 SERVINGS

½ cup diced cucumber

¾ teaspoon salt, divided

1 cup plain nonfat Greek yogurt

2 tablespoons fresh lemon juice, divided

1 teaspoon grated lemon peel, divided

1 teaspoon minced garlic, divided

¼ teaspoon black pepper

4 skinless salmon fillets (4 ounces each)

1. Place cucumber in small colander set over small bowl; sprinkle with ¼ teaspoon salt. Drain 1 hour.

2. For tzatziki sauce, stir yogurt, cucumber, 1 tablespoon lemon juice, ½ teaspoon lemon peel, ½ teaspoon garlic and ¼ teaspoon salt in small bowl until combined. Cover and refrigerate until ready to use.

3. Combine remaining 1 tablespoon lemon juice, ½ teaspoon lemon peel, ½ teaspoon garlic, ¼ teaspoon salt and pepper in small bowl; mix well. Rub evenly onto salmon.

4. Heat nonstick grill pan over medium-high heat. Cook salmon 5 minutes per side or until fish begins to flake when tested with fork. Serve with tzatziki sauce.

**SERVING SUGGESTION:** Serve this Mediterranean-inspired dish with fresh vegetables or a savory salad, if desired.

# SEARED SCALLOPS OVER GARLIC-LEMON SPINACH

MAKES 4 SERVINGS

1 tablespoon olive oil

1 pound sea scallops*
(approximately 12)

¼ teaspoon salt

⅛ teaspoon black pepper

2 cloves garlic, minced

1 shallot, minced

1 package (6 ounces) baby
spinach

1 tablespoon fresh lemon
juice

Lemon wedges (optional)

*Make sure scallops are dry before
putting them in the pan so they can
get a golden crust.*

1. Heat oil in large nonstick skillet over medium-high heat. Add scallops; sprinkle with salt and pepper. Cook 2 to 3 minutes per side or until golden. Remove to large plate; keep warm.

2. Add garlic and shallot to skillet; cook and stir 45 seconds or until fragrant. Add spinach; cook 2 minutes or until spinach just begins to wilt, stirring occasionally. Remove from heat; stir in lemon juice.

3. Serve scallops over spinach. Garnish with lemon wedges.

# MEDITERRANEAN RED SNAPPER

**MAKES 4 SERVINGS**

1 to 1½ pounds red snapper fillets (4 to 5 ounces each)

4 sheets (18×12 inches each) heavy-duty foil, lightly sprayed with nonstick cooking spray

8 sun-dried tomatoes, packed in oil, drained and chopped

⅓ cup sliced pitted black olives

1½ teaspoons minced garlic

½ teaspoon dried oregano

½ teaspoon dried marjoram

¼ teaspoon black pepper

⅛ teaspoon salt

Hot cooked rice (optional)

Sautéed vegetables (optional)

1. Prepare grill for direct cooking.

2. Rinse fish under cold running water; pat dry with paper towels. Place 1 fish fillet in center of 1 sheet of foil. Repeat with remaining fish and foil.

3. Combine sun-dried tomatoes, olives, garlic, oregano, marjoram, pepper and salt in small bowl. Sprinkle over fish.

4. Double-fold sides and ends of foil to seal packets, leaving head space for heat circulation. Place packets on baking sheet.

5. Slide packets off baking sheet onto grill grid. Grill, covered, over medium-high coals 9 to 11 minutes or until fish flakes with fork. Carefully open one end of each packet to allow steam to escape. Open packets and transfer mixture to serving plates. Serve with rice and vegetables, if desired.

# MEDITERRANEAN SHRIMP AND BEAN SALAD

MAKES 4 SERVINGS

10 ounces large cooked shrimp, cut into bite-size pieces

1½ cups grape or cherry tomatoes, halved

1 large shallot, minced

¾ cup canned no-salt-added chickpeas

¼ cup shredded fresh basil

¼ teaspoon paprika

¼ teaspoon salt (optional)

¼ teaspoon black pepper

⅛ teaspoon dried oregano

3 tablespoons low-sodium tomato or vegetable juice

1 tablespoon white wine vinegar

1 tablespoon olive oil

Combine shrimp, tomatoes, shallot, chickpeas and basil in large bowl. Stir together paprika, salt, if desired, pepper and oregano in small bowl. Gradually stir in tomato juice. Stir in vinegar and oil. Pour over shrimp mixture; toss gently to coat.

# GREEK-STYLE SALMON

MAKES 4 SERVINGS

1½ teaspoons olive oil

1¾ cups diced tomatoes, drained

6 pitted black olives, coarsely chopped

4 pitted green olives, coarsely chopped

3 tablespoons lemon juice

2 tablespoons chopped fresh Italian parsley

1 tablespoon capers, rinsed and drained

2 medium cloves garlic, thinly sliced

¼ teaspoon black pepper

1 pound salmon fillets

1. Heat oil in large skillet over medium heat. Add tomatoes, olives, lemon juice, parsley, capers, garlic and pepper; bring to a simmer, stirring frequently. Cook 5 minutes or until reduced by about one third, stirring occasionally.

2. Rinse salmon and pat dry with paper towels. Push sauce to one side of skillet. Add salmon; spoon sauce over salmon. Cover; cook 10 to 15 minutes or until salmon begins to flake when tested with fork.

# ORZO RISOTTO WITH SHRIMP AND VEGETABLES

MAKES 4 SERVINGS

1 zucchini, halved and sliced

2 teaspoons grated lemon peel

1 cup sliced mushrooms

½ cup chopped onion

2 cloves garlic

¾ teaspoon dried sage

¼ to ½ teaspoon dried thyme

1¼ cups uncooked orzo pasta

2 cans (about 14 ounces each) fat-free reduced-sodium chicken broth

8 ounces raw shrimp, peeled and deveined (with tails on)

¾ cup frozen peas, thawed

¼ cup grated Parmesan cheese

Salt and black pepper

1. Spray large saucepan with nonstick cooking spray; heat over medium heat. Add zucchini and lemon peel; cook and stir 2 to 3 minutes or until zucchini is tender. Remove to bowl.

2. Add mushrooms, onion, garlic, sage and thyme to saucepan; cook and stir 3 minutes or until onion is tender. Add orzo; cook and stir until lightly browned.

3. Bring broth to a boil in medium saucepan; keep warm over low heat. Add broth to orzo mixture, ½ cup at a time, stirring constantly until broth is absorbed before adding next ½ cup. Continue cooking 10 to 15 minutes or until orzo is tender.

4. Stir shrimp and peas into orzo mixture during last half of cooking time. Stir in zucchini mixture during last 2 to 3 minutes of cooking time. Stir in Parmesan cheese; season with salt and pepper.

# MEDITERRANEAN TUNA SALAD

MAKES 4 SERVINGS

1 cup diced tomato

1 tablespoon olive oil

1 tablespoon lemon juice

2 teaspoons Dijon mustard

1 clove garlic, minced

¼ teaspoon salt

¼ teaspoon dried basil

2 cans (6 ounces each) solid white tuna packed in water, drained and flaked

½ cup diced celery

⅓ cup chopped fresh basil

Red leaf lettuce leaves

½ pound steamed green beans

1 medium red bell pepper, cut into strips

8 cherry tomatoes, halved

1. Combine diced tomato, oil, lemon juice, mustard, garlic, salt and dried basil in large bowl; let stand 5 minutes. Stir in tuna, celery and fresh basil. Refrigerate, covered, 1 to 2 hours to allow flavors to blend, stirring once.

2. Line serving platter with lettuce leaves. Mound tuna salad in center; serve with green beans, bell pepper and cherry tomatoes.

# GRILLED SWORDFISH SICILIAN STYLE

MAKES 4 TO 6 SERVINGS

- 3 tablespoons extra virgin olive oil
- 1 clove garlic, minced
- 2 tablespoons lemon juice
- ¾ teaspoon salt
- ⅛ teaspoon black pepper
- 3 tablespoons capers, drained
- 1 tablespoon chopped fresh oregano or basil
- 1½ pounds swordfish steaks (¾ inch thick)

1. Oil grill grid. Prepare grill for direct cooking.

2. For sauce, heat oil in small saucepan over low heat; add garlic. Cook 1 minute. Remove from heat; cool slightly. Whisk in lemon juice, salt and pepper until salt is dissolved. Stir in capers and oregano.

3. Place swordfish on grid over medium heat. Grill 7 to 8 minutes or until centers are opaque, turning once. Serve fish with sauce.

# GRILLED TUNA NIÇOISE WITH CITRUS MARINADE

MAKES 4 SERVINGS

Citrus Marinade (recipe follows)

1 tuna steak (about 1 pound)

2 cups fresh green beans

4 cups romaine lettuce leaves, washed and torn

8 small red potatoes, cooked and quartered

1 cup chopped seeded fresh tomato

4 cooked egg whites, chopped

¼ cup red onion slices, halved

2 teaspoons chopped black olives

Prepared fat-free salad dressing (optional)

1. Prepare Citrus Marinade; combine with tuna in large resealable food storage bag. Seal bag; turn to coat. Marinate in refrigerator 1 hour, turning occasionally.

2. Prepare grill for direct cooking. Drain tuna; discard marinade. Grill 8 to 10 minutes or until tuna begins to flake when tested with fork, turning once. (Or broil tuna 4 inches from heat, 8 to 10 minutes, turning once.) Slice tuna into ¼-inch-thick slices; set aside.

3. Place 2 cups water in large saucepan; bring to a boil over high heat. Add green beans; cook 2 minutes. Drain; rinse with cold water and drain again.

4. Place lettuce on large serving platter. Arrange tuna, green beans, potatoes, tomato, egg whites and onion on lettuce. Sprinkle each serving with olives. Serve with fat-free salad dressing, if desired.

# CITRUS MARINADE

½ cup fresh lime juice

¼ cup vegetable oil

2 green onions, chopped

1 teaspoon dried tarragon

¼ teaspoon garlic powder

¼ teaspoon black pepper

Blend all ingredients in small bowl.

# FRESH GARLIC SHRIMP LINGUINE

MAKES 4 SERVINGS

6 ounces uncooked multigrain linguine or spaghetti, broken in half

½ pound raw shrimp, peeled and deveined

¼ cup grated Parmesan cheese

3 tablespoons margarine

1 clove garlic, minced

½ teaspoon seafood seasoning

¼ cup finely chopped fresh parsley (optional)

⅛ teaspoon salt (optional)

1. Cook linguine according to package directions, omitting salt and fat, about 7 minutes or until al dente. Add shrimp; cook 3 to 4 minutes or until shrimp are pink and opaque. Drain; transfer to medium bowl.

2. Add Parmesan cheese, margarine, garlic and seafood seasoning; toss gently to coat. Add parsley and salt, if desired; toss to combine.

# ROASTED SALMON WITH HORSERADISH ROSEMARY AIOLI

MAKES 4 SERVINGS

4 salmon fillets (6 ounces each), rinsed and patted dry

2 teaspoons extra virgin olive oil

½ teaspoon coarsely ground black pepper

⅛ teaspoon salt

½ cup mayonnaise

¼ cup sour cream

½ teaspoon minced garlic

2 to 3 teaspoons prepared horseradish

¼ teaspoon dried rosemary

1 teaspoon Dijon mustard

1. Preheat oven to 400°F. Line baking sheet with heavy-duty foil; spray lightly with nonstick cooking spray. Set aside.

2. Rub both sides of fillets with oil. Sprinkle evenly with pepper and salt. Press seasonings to adhere. Arrange fillets on prepared baking sheet. Bake 12 minutes or until opaque in center.

3. Meanwhile, in small bowl, combine remaining ingredients. Top each fillet with equal amounts of sauce.

NOTE: The sauce may be made up to 1 week in advance. Cover and store in refrigerator.

# TERIYAKI SHRIMP AND MANGO KABOBS OVER ORZO

MAKES 4 SERVINGS

¼ cup reduced-sodium teriyaki sauce

10 ounces large raw shrimp (21 to 25 per pound), peeled and deveined

14 cherry tomatoes, divided

1 mango, cut into chunks

9 green onions, trimmed and cut into 2-inch pieces

1½ cups reduced-sodium chicken broth

½ cup water

1 cup uncooked orzo pasta

1 clove garlic, minced

4 cups fresh baby spinach

½ teaspoon black pepper

1. Preheat grill to medium-high heat.

2. Pour teriyaki sauce in large resealable food storage bag. Place shrimp in bag; refrigerate at least 1 hour. Remove shrimp and reserve remaining teriyaki sauce.

3. Make 4 kabobs, starting with 1 cherry tomato then alternating with 1 shrimp, 1 mango and 1 green onion; end with 1 cherry tomato. Brush remaining teriyaki sauce over kabobs. Grill kabobs, turning once until shrimp are pink and opaque, about 8 to 10 minutes total.

4. Meanwhile dice remaining 6 cherry tomatoes; set aside. In large saucepan combine broth, water, orzo and garlic in large saucepan. Bring to a boil; cover and reduce heat to medium-low. Cook 10 minutes, stir in spinach, tomatoes and pepper. Cook 2 to 3 minutes or until spinach is wilted and orzo is cooked through. Serve shrimp kabobs over orzo.

TIP: To reduce the sodium in this recipe, omit the chicken broth and cook orzo in 2 cups of water.

# HEARTY & SIDE SALADS

## FARRO, CHICKPEA AND SPINACH SALAD

MAKES 8 TO 12 SERVINGS

1 cup uncooked pearled farro

3 cups baby spinach, stemmed

1 medium cucumber, chopped

1 can (about 15 ounces) chickpeas, rinsed and drained

¾ cup pitted kalamata olives

¼ cup extra virgin olive oil

3 tablespoons white or golden balsamic vinegar *or* 3 tablespoons cider vinegar mixed with ½ teaspoon sugar

1 teaspoon chopped fresh rosemary

1 clove garlic, minced

1 teaspoon salt

⅛ to ¼ teaspoon red pepper flakes (optional)

½ cup (2 ounces) crumbled goat or feta cheese

1. Bring 4 cups water to a boil in medium saucepan. Add farro; reduce heat and simmer 20 to 25 minutes or until farro is tender. Drain and rinse under cold water until cool.

2. Meanwhile, combine spinach, cucumber, chickpeas, olives, oil, vinegar, rosemary, garlic, salt and red pepper flakes, if desired, in large bowl. Stir in farro until well blended. Add goat cheese; stir gently.

# GREEK LENTIL SALAD WITH FETA VINAIGRETTE

MAKES 3 SERVINGS

4 cups water

¾ cup uncooked lentils

1 bay leaf

¼ cup chopped green onions

1 large stalk celery, chopped

1 cup grape tomatoes, halved

¼ cup (1 ounce) crumbled feta cheese

2 tablespoons olive oil

1 tablespoon white wine vinegar

½ teaspoon dried thyme

½ teaspoon dried oregano

½ teaspoon salt

¼ teaspoon black pepper

1. Combine water, lentils and bay leaf in small saucepan. Bring to a boil. Reduce heat to medium-low; partially cover and cook 40 minutes or until lentils are tender but not mushy.

2. Drain lentils; remove and discard bay leaf. Place lentils in serving bowl; stir in green onions, celery and tomatoes.

3. Combine feta cheese, oil, vinegar, thyme, oregano, salt and pepper in small bowl. Pour over salad; gently stir until blended. Let stand at least 10 minutes before serving to allow flavors to blend.

# MARINATED TOMATO SALAD

MAKES 8 SERVINGS

1½ cups white wine or tarragon vinegar

½ teaspoon salt

¼ cup finely chopped shallots

2 tablespoons finely chopped fresh chives

2 tablespoons fresh lemon juice

¼ teaspoon white pepper

2 tablespoons extra virgin olive oil

6 plum tomatoes, quartered

2 large yellow tomatoes,* sliced horizontally into ½-inch-thick slices

16 red cherry tomatoes, halved

16 small yellow pear tomatoes,* halved (optional)

Sunflower sprouts (optional)

*Substitute 10 plum tomatoes, quartered, for yellow tomatoes and yellow pear tomatoes, if desired.

1. Combine vinegar and salt in large bowl; stir until salt is completely dissolved. Add shallots, chives, lemon juice and pepper; mix well. Slowly whisk in oil until well blended.

2. Add tomatoes to marinade; toss well. Cover; let stand at room temperature 30 minutes or up to 2 hours before serving.

3. To serve, divide salad equally among eight plates. Garnish with sunflower sprouts.

# PESTO FARRO SALAD WITH PEAS, ASPARAGUS AND FETA

MAKES 4 SERVINGS

- **1 cup uncooked pearled farro**
- **1 cup peas**
- **1 bunch asparagus, trimmed and cut into 1-inch pieces**
- **2 cups fresh packed basil leaves**
- **½ cup packed fresh Italian parsley**
- **¼ cup toasted walnuts**
- **2 cloves garlic**
- **½ cup extra virgin olive oil**
- **½ cup grated Parmesan cheese**
- **Coarse salt and black pepper**
- **½ cup (2 ounces) crumbled feta cheese**

**1.** Bring large saucepan of water to a boil over high heat. Add farro; reduce heat to medium-low. Cook about 30 minutes or until tender, adding peas during last 5 minutes of cooking time and asparagus during last 2 minutes of cooking time. Drain well.

**2.** Meanwhile, place basil, parsley, walnuts and garlic in food processor. Pulse until coarsely chopped. With motor running, add oil in thin, steady stream. Add Parmesan cheese; pulse to combine. Season with salt and pepper.

**3.** Transfer farro mixture to large bowl. Add ¾ cup pesto mixture; toss to coat. (Reserve remaining pesto for another use.) Add feta cheese; stir until combined. Season with additional salt and pepper, if desired.

# BEET AND ARUGULA SALAD

MAKES 6 TO 8 SERVINGS

8 medium beets (5 to 6 ounces each)

⅓ cup red wine vinegar

¾ teaspoon salt

½ teaspoon black pepper

3 tablespoons extra virgin olive oil

1 package (5 ounces) baby arugula

1 package (4 ounces) crumbled goat cheese with garlic and herbs

1. Place beets in large saucepan; add water to cover by 2 inches. Bring to a boil over medium-high heat. Reduce heat to medium-low; cover and simmer 30 minutes or until beets can be easily pierced with tip of knife. Drain well; set aside until cool enough to handle.

2. Meanwhile, whisk vinegar, salt and pepper in large bowl. Slowly add oil in thin, steady stream, whisking until well blended. Remove 3 tablespoons dressing to medium bowl.

3. Peel beets and cut into wedges. Add warm beets to large bowl; toss to coat with dressing. Add arugula to medium bowl; toss gently to coat with dressing. Place arugula on platter or plates, top with beets and goat cheese.

# GREEK CHICKPEA SALAD

MAKES 4 SERVINGS

4 cups packed baby spinach

1 cup canned chickpeas, rinsed and drained

1 large shallot, thinly sliced

4 pitted kalamata olives, sliced

2 tablespoons crumbled reduced-fat feta cheese

¼ cup plain nonfat Greek yogurt

2 teaspoons white wine vinegar

1 small clove garlic, minced

1 teaspoon olive oil

¼ teaspoon black pepper

⅛ teaspoon salt

1. Combine spinach, chickpeas, shallot, olives and feta cheese in large bowl; toss gently.

2. Whisk yogurt, vinegar, garlic, oil, pepper and salt in small bowl until well blended. Add to salad just before serving; toss gently.

# GREEK-STYLE CUCUMBER SALAD

MAKES 4 SERVINGS

1 medium cucumber, peeled and diced

¼ cup chopped green onions

1 teaspoon minced fresh dill

1 small clove garlic, minced

1 cup sour cream or sour half-and-half

½ teaspoon salt

¼ teaspoon black pepper

⅛ teaspoon ground cumin

Lemon juice (optional)

1. Place cucumber, green onions, dill and garlic in salad bowl.

2. Combine sour cream, salt, pepper and cumin in small bowl; stir until blended. Stir sour cream mixture into cucumber mixture. Sprinkle with lemon juice to taste, if desired.

# LENTIL AND ORZO PASTA SALAD

MAKES 4 SERVINGS

8 cups water

½ cup dried lentils, rinsed and sorted

4 ounces uncooked orzo pasta

1½ cups quartered cherry tomatoes, sweet grape variety

¾ cup finely chopped celery

½ cup chopped red onion

2 ounces pitted olives (about 16 olives), coarsely chopped

3 to 4 tablespoons cider vinegar

1 tablespoon olive oil

1 tablespoon dried basil

1 medium clove garlic, minced

⅛ teaspoon red pepper flakes

1 package (4 ounces) crumbled feta cheese with sun-dried tomatoes and basil

1. Bring water to a boil in Dutch oven over high heat. Add lentils; boil 12 minutes.

2. Add orzo. Cook 10 minutes or just until tender; drain. Rinse under cold running water to cool completely; drain well.

3. Meanwhile, combine remaining ingredients except feta cheese in large bowl; set aside.

4. Add lentil mixture to tomato mixture; toss gently to blend. Add feta cheese; toss gently. Let stand 15 minutes before serving.

# VEGGIE SALAD WITH WHITE BEANS AND FETA CHEESE

MAKES 4 SERVINGS

- 1 can (about 15 ounces) navy beans, rinsed and drained
- 1 can (14 ounces) quartered artichoke hearts, drained
- 1 medium green bell pepper, chopped
- 1 yellow bell pepper, chopped
- 1 cup grape tomatoes, halved
- ¼ cup chopped fresh basil *or* 1½ tablespoons dried basil plus ¼ cup chopped fresh parsley
- ¼ cup extra virgin olive oil
- 3 to 4 tablespoons red wine vinegar
- 1 clove garlic, minced
- 1 teaspoon Dijon mustard
- ½ teaspoon black pepper
- ¼ teaspoon salt
- 1 package (4 ounces) crumbled feta cheese with sun-dried tomatoes and basil
- 1 package (about 5 ounces) spring greens mix (optional)

1. Combine beans, artichokes, bell peppers, tomatoes, basil, oil, vinegar, garlic, mustard, black pepper and salt in large bowl; toss gently. Fold in feta cheese. Let stand 10 minutes.

2. Place greens on four serving plates, if desired. Top with vegetable mixture.

# GREEK RICE SALAD

MAKES 4 SERVINGS

1 cup water

¾ cup uncooked instant brown rice

1 cup packed baby spinach

⅔ cup quartered cherry tomatoes

1 tablespoon lemon juice

2 teaspoons extra virgin olive oil

1½ teaspoons Greek seasoning

¼ teaspoon salt

⅛ teaspoon black pepper

¼ cup pine nuts

1. Bring water to a boil in small saucepan over high heat; add rice. Return to a boil. Reduce heat and simmer, covered, 5 minutes. Remove from heat and let stand 5 minutes. Rinse rice under cold water until cool; drain.

2. Combine spinach, tomatoes and rice in medium bowl. Whisk together, lemon juice, oil, Greek seasoning, salt and pepper in small bowl.

3. Pour juice mixture over spinach mixture; toss to blend. Serve immediately or refrigerate until ready to serve. Sprinkle with pine nuts.

# TOMATO, AVOCADO AND CUCUMBER SALAD WITH FETA CHEESE

MAKES 4 SERVINGS

1½ tablespoons extra virgin olive oil

1 tablespoon balsamic vinegar

1 clove garlic, minced

¼ teaspoon salt

¼ teaspoon black pepper

2 cups diced seeded plum tomatoes

1 small ripe avocado, diced into ½-inch chunks

½ cup chopped cucumber

⅓ cup crumbled reduced-fat feta cheese

4 large red leaf lettuce leaves

Chopped fresh basil (optional)

1. Whisk oil, vinegar, garlic, salt and pepper in medium bowl. Add tomatoes and avocado; toss gently to coat. Stir in cucumber and feta cheese.

2. Arrange 1 lettuce leaf on each serving plate. Spoon salad evenly onto lettuce leaves. Top with basil, if desired.

# ORZO, BLACK BEAN AND EDAMAME SALAD

**MAKES 4 SERVINGS**

- ⅔ cup uncooked orzo pasta
- ¾ cup frozen shelled edamame
- ¾ cup diced carrots
- ¾ cup canned black beans, rinsed and drained
- ½ cup diced green bell pepper
- 2 to 3 tablespoons lime juice
- 1 tablespoon extra virgin olive oil
- ¼ teaspoon kosher salt
- ⅛ teaspoon black pepper
- 2 tablespoons finely chopped fresh cilantro
- 2 tablespoons grated Parmesan cheese

1. Cook orzo according to package directions, omitting any salt or fat. Add edamame and carrots to saucepan about 5 minutes before end of cooking time; continue cooking until orzo is tender. Drain, transfer to large bowl; add black beans and bell pepper.

2. Whisk lime juice, oil, salt and black pepper in small bowl. Pour over salad, sprinkle with cilantro and top with Parmesan cheese; toss gently. Serve lukewarm.

NOTE: Edamame are fresh green soybeans. They're usually available in the frozen section of the supermarket with or without their pods.

# GREEK SALAD

MAKES 6 SERVINGS

### SALAD

- 3 medium tomatoes, cut into 8 wedges each and seeds removed
- 1 green bell pepper, cut into 1-inch pieces
- ½ English cucumber (8 to 10 inches), quartered lengthwise and sliced crosswise
- ½ red onion, thinly sliced
- ½ cup pitted kalamata olives
- 1 block (8 ounces) feta cheese, cut into ½-inch cubes

### DRESSING

- 6 tablespoons extra virgin olive oil
- 3 tablespoons red wine vinegar
- 1 to 2 cloves garlic, minced
- ¾ teaspoon dried oregano
- ¾ teaspoon salt
- ¼ teaspoon black pepper

1. Combine tomatoes, bell pepper, cucumber, onion and olives in large bowl. Top with feta cheese.

2. For dressing, whisk oil, vinegar, garlic, oregano, salt and black pepper in medium bowl until well blended. Pour over salad; stir gently to coat.

# SPRING GREENS WITH BLUEBERRIES, WALNUTS AND FETA CHEESE

MAKES 4 SERVINGS

1 tablespoon canola oil

1 tablespoon white wine vinegar or sherry vinegar

2 teaspoons Dijon mustard

½ teaspoon salt (optional)

½ teaspoon black pepper

5 cups mixed spring greens (5 ounces)

1 cup fresh blueberries

½ cup (2 ounces) crumbled reduced-fat feta cheese

¼ cup chopped walnuts or pecans, toasted*

*To toast nuts, place in nonstick skillet. Cook and stir over medium-low heat about 5 minutes or until nuts begin to brown. Remove immediately to plate to cool.

1. Whisk oil, vinegar, mustard, salt, if desired, and pepper in large bowl.

2. Add greens and blueberries; toss gently to coat. Top with feta cheese and walnuts. Serve immediately.

# GRAINS, VEGGIES & SIDES

## LENTILS WITH PASTA

MAKES 6 TO 8 SERVINGS

1 cup dried lentils

1 cup dried split peas

1 tablespoon olive oil

1 onion, chopped

2 tablespoons tomato paste

2 cloves garlic, minced

1 teaspoon salt

¼ teaspoon black pepper

1 can (about 14 ounces) diced tomatoes

3 cups water

12 ounces uncooked short pasta (elbow macaroni, small shells, ditalini or similar)

Shredded Romano or Parmesan cheese (optional)

1. Place lentils and split peas in medium bowl; cover with water. Let stand at least 10 minutes.

2. Heat oil in large saucepan or Dutch oven over medium heat. Add onion; cook and stir 5 minutes or until onion is lightly browned. Add tomato paste, garlic, salt and pepper; cook and stir 1 minute. Add tomatoes and 3 cups water; bring to a boil.

3. Drain lentils and split peas; add to saucepan. Reduce heat to medium-low; cover and simmer about 40 minutes or until lentils and split peas are tender.

4. Meanwhile, cook pasta in large saucepan of boiling salted water according to package directions for al dente. Drain and add to lentil mixture; mix well. Serve with Romano cheese, if desired.

# SPICED CHICKPEAS & COUSCOUS

**MAKES 6 SERVINGS**

1 can (about 14 ounces) vegetable broth

1 teaspoon ground coriander

½ teaspoon ground cardamom

½ teaspoon ground turmeric

½ teaspoon hot pepper sauce

¼ teaspoon salt

⅛ teaspoon ground cinnamon

1 cup matchstick-size carrots

1 can (about 15 ounces) chickpeas, rinsed and drained

1 cup frozen green peas

1 cup quick-cooking couscous

2 tablespoons chopped fresh mint or parsley

1. Combine broth, coriander, cardamom, turmeric, hot pepper sauce, salt and cinnamon in large saucepan; bring to a boil over high heat. Add carrots; reduce heat and simmer 5 minutes.

2. Add chickpeas and green peas; return to a simmer. Simmer, uncovered, 2 minutes.

3. Stir in couscous. Cover; remove from heat. Let stand 5 minutes or until liquid is absorbed. Sprinkle with mint.

# SWEET & SAVORY SWEET POTATO SALAD

**MAKES 6 SERVINGS**

- 4 cups peeled chopped cooked sweet potatoes (about 4 to 6)
- ¾ cup chopped green onions
- ½ cup chopped fresh parsley
- ½ cup dried unsweetened cherries
- ¼ cup plus 2 tablespoons rice wine vinegar
- 2 tablespoons coarse ground mustard
- 1 tablespoon extra virgin olive oil
- ¾ teaspoon garlic powder
- ¼ teaspoon black pepper
- ⅛ teaspoon salt

1. Combine sweet potatoes, green onions, parsley and cherries in large bowl; mix gently.

2. Whisk vinegar, mustard, oil, garlic powder, pepper and salt in small bowl until well blended. Pour over sweet potato mixture; toss gently to coat. Serve immediately or cover and refrigerate until ready to serve.

# TABBOULEH IN TOMATO CUPS

**MAKES 8 SERVINGS**

4 large firm ripe tomatoes
   (about 8 ounces each)

2 tablespoons olive oil

4 green onions with tops,
   thinly sliced diagonally

1 cup uncooked bulgur
   wheat

1 cup water

2 tablespoons lemon juice

1 tablespoon chopped fresh
   mint leaves *or*
   ½ teaspoon dried mint

Salt and black pepper

Lemon peel and chopped
   mint leaves (optional)

**1.** Cut tomatoes in half crosswise. Scoop pulp and seeds out of tomatoes into medium bowl, leaving ¼-inch-thick shells.

**2.** Invert tomatoes on paper towel-lined plate; drain 20 minutes. Chop tomato pulp; set aside.

**3.** Heat oil in medium saucepan over medium-high heat. Cook and stir white parts of onions 1 to 2 minutes until wilted. Add bulgur; cook 3 to 5 minutes until browned.

**4.** Add reserved tomato pulp, water, lemon juice and 1 tablespoon fresh mint to bulgur mixture. Bring to a boil over high heat; reduce heat to medium-low. Cover; simmer gently 15 to 20 minutes until liquid is absorbed.

**5.** Set aside a few sliced green onion tops for garnish; stir remaining green onions into bulgur mixture. Season with salt and pepper. Spoon mixture into tomato cups.*

**6.** Preheat oven to 400°F. Place filled cups in 13×9-inch baking dish; bake 15 minutes or until heated through. Top with reserved onion tops. Garnish with lemon peel and mint leaves. Serve immediately.

*Tomato cups may be covered and refrigerated at this point up to 24 hours.*

# GREEN BEANS WITH GARLIC-CILANTRO BUTTER

MAKES 4 TO 6 SERVINGS

1½ pounds green beans, trimmed

3 tablespoons butter

1 red bell pepper, cut into thin strips

½ sweet onion, halved and thinly sliced

2 teaspoons minced garlic

1 teaspoon salt

2 tablespoons chopped fresh cilantro

Black pepper

1. Bring large saucepan of salted water to a boil over medium-high heat. Add beans; cook 6 minutes or until tender. Drain beans.

2. Meanwhile, melt butter in large skillet over medium-high heat. Add bell pepper and onion; cook and stir 3 minutes or until vegetables are tender but not browned. Add garlic; cook and stir 30 seconds. Add beans and salt; cook and stir 2 minutes or until beans are heated through and coated with butter. Stir in cilantro; season with black pepper. Serve immediately.

# ROSEMARY, HARICOTS VERTS AND GOAT CHEESE QUINOA

MAKES 6 SERVINGS

- 1 cup tri-colored uncooked quinoa
- 2 cups vegetable broth
- 1 tablespoon chopped fresh rosemary
- 1 package (12 ounces) fresh haricots verts, cut in half
- 3 tablespoons olive oil
- 1 tablespoon Dijon mustard
- 1 teaspoon honey
- 1 tablespoon fresh lemon juice
- ¼ teaspoon salt
- ⅛ teaspoon black pepper
- ½ cup toasted pecan pieces
- 1 container (4 ounces) crumbled goat cheese

1. Place quinoa in fine-mesh strainer; rinse well under cold running water.

2. Combine quinoa and broth in medium saucepan; bring to a boil over high heat. Reduce heat to low; cover and simmer 15 to 20 minutes or until quinoa is tender and broth is absorbed. Add rosemary and haricots verts during last 5 minutes of cooking. Remove from heat; cool.

3. Meanwhile, combine oil, mustard, honey, lemon juice, salt and pepper in small bowl; set aside.

4. Place cooled quinoa mixture in large bowl. Toss with dressing and pecans. Sprinkle with goat cheese before serving.

# MEDITERRANEAN ORZO AND VEGETABLE PILAF

MAKES 6 SERVINGS

4 ounces (½ cup plus 2 tablespoons) uncooked orzo pasta

2 teaspoons olive oil

1 small onion, diced

2 cloves garlic, minced

1 small zucchini, diced

½ cup (2 ounces) fat-free reduced-sodium chicken broth

1 can (about 14 ounces) artichoke hearts, drained and quartered

1 medium tomato, chopped

½ teaspoon dried oregano

½ teaspoon salt

¼ teaspoon black pepper

½ cup (2 ounces) crumbled feta cheese

Sliced black pitted olives (optional)

1. Cook orzo according to package directions, omitting salt and fat. Drain.

2. Heat oil in large nonstick skillet over medium heat. Add onion; cook and stir 5 minutes or until translucent. Add garlic; cook and stir 1 minute. Reduce heat to low. Add zucchini and broth; simmer 5 minutes or until zucchini is crisp-tender.

3. Add cooked orzo, artichokes, tomato, oregano, salt and pepper; cook and stir 1 minute or until heated through. Top with feta cheese and olives, if desired.

# GREEK SPINACH-CHEESE ROLLS

**MAKES 15 SERVINGS**

- 1 loaf (1 pound) frozen bread dough, thawed according to package directions
- 1 package (10 ounces) frozen chopped spinach, thawed and squeezed dry
- ¾ cup (3 ounces) crumbled feta cheese
- ½ cup (2 ounces) shredded reduced-fat Monterey Jack cheese
- 4 green onions, thinly sliced
- 1 teaspoon dried dill weed
- ½ teaspoon garlic powder
- ½ teaspoon black pepper

1. Spray 15 standard (2½-inch) muffin cups with nonstick cooking spray; set aside. Roll out dough into 15×9-inch rectangle on lightly floured surface. (If dough is springy and difficult to roll, cover with plastic wrap and let rest 5 minutes.)

2. Combine spinach, feta cheese, Monterey Jack cheese, green onions, dill, garlic powder and pepper in large bowl; mix well. Spread spinach mixture evenly over dough, leaving 1-inch border on long sides.

3. Starting with long side, roll up tightly jelly-roll style; pinch seam to seal. Place roll seam side down on work surface; cut crosswise into 15 slices with serrated knife. Place slices cut sides up in prepared muffin cups. Cover with plastic wrap; let stand in warm place 30 minutes or until dough is slightly puffy. Preheat oven to 375°F.

4. Bake 20 to 25 minutes or until golden brown. Serve warm or at room temperature. Rolls can be stored in airtight container in refrigerator up to 2 days.

# MEDITERRANEAN-STYLE ROASTED VEGETABLES

**MAKES 6 SERVINGS**

1½ pounds red potatoes, cut into ½-inch chunks

1 tablespoon plus 1½ teaspoons olive oil, divided

1 red bell pepper, cut into ½-inch pieces

1 yellow or orange bell pepper, cut into ½-inch pieces

1 small red onion, cut into ½-inch wedges

2 cloves garlic, minced

½ teaspoon salt

¼ teaspoon black pepper

1 tablespoon balsamic vinegar

¼ cup chopped fresh basil leaves

1. Preheat oven to 425°F. Spray large roasting pan with nonstick cooking spray.

2. Place potatoes in prepared pan. Drizzle with 1 tablespoon oil; toss to coat evenly. Roast 10 minutes.

3. Add bell peppers and onion to pan. Drizzle with remaining 1½ teaspoons oil. Sprinkle with garlic, salt and black pepper; toss to coat evenly.

4. Roast 18 to 20 minutes or until vegetables are browned and tender, stirring once.

5. Transfer vegetables to large serving dish. Drizzle vinegar over vegetables; toss to coat evenly. Add basil; toss again. Serve warm or at room temperature.

# LENTILS WITH WALNUTS

MAKES 4 TO 6 SERVINGS

1 cup brown lentils

1 very small onion or large shallot, chopped

1 stalk celery, trimmed and chopped

1 large carrot, chopped

¼ teaspoon dried thyme

3 cups chicken broth

Salt and black pepper, to taste

¼ cup chopped walnuts

**SLOW COOKER DIRECTIONS**

1. Combine lentils, onion, celery, carrot, thyme and broth in 4-quart slow cooker. Cover; cook on HIGH 3 hours. *Do not overcook.* (Lentils should absorb most or all of broth. Slightly tilt slow cooker to check.)

2. Season with salt and pepper. Spoon lentils into serving bowl and sprinkle with walnuts.

# GREEK PASTA SALAD

**MAKES 8 SERVINGS**

6 cups cooked multigrain or whole wheat rotini or penne pasta

1½ cups diced cucumber

2 medium tomatoes, diced

1 medium green bell pepper, diced

½ cup (2 ounces) crumbled feta cheese

12 medium pitted black olives, sliced into thirds

¼ cup chopped fresh dill

Juice of ½ lemon

¼ teaspoon salt

⅛ teaspoon black pepper

1. Combine pasta, cucumber, tomatoes, bell pepper, feta cheese, olives and dill in large bowl.

2. Whisk lemon juice, salt and pepper in small bowl. Toss with pasta mixture.

3. Cover and refrigerate until ready to serve.

# BROWN RICE WITH CHICKPEAS, SPINACH AND FETA

MAKES 4 SERVINGS

½ cup diced celery

½ cup uncooked instant brown rice

1 can (about 15 ounces) reduced-fat chickpeas, rinsed and drained

1 clove garlic, minced (optional)

1 package (10 ounces) frozen chopped spinach, thawed and squeezed dry

1 teaspoon Greek or Italian seasoning

¾ teaspoon vegetable broth

¼ teaspoon salt (optional)

⅛ teaspoon black pepper

2 cups water

1 tablespoon lemon juice

½ cup (2 ounces) crumbled reduced-fat feta cheese

1. Heat large skillet coated with nonstick cooking spray over medium-high heat. Add celery; cook, stirring occasionally, 4 minutes or until lightly glazed and brown in spots.

2. Add rice, chickpeas, garlic, if desired, spinach, Greek seasoning, broth, salt, if desired, pepper and water. Stir to combine. Cover and bring to a gentle boil. Reduce heat to low and boil gently 12 minutes or until rice is tender. Remove from heat; add lemon juice and feta cheese. Mix gently with large spoon.

# BULGUR PILAF WITH CARAMELIZED ONIONS & KALE

MAKES 6 SERVINGS

1 tablespoon olive oil

1 small onion, cut into thin wedges

1 clove garlic, minced

2 cups chopped kale

2 cups fat-free reduced-sodium vegetable or chicken broth

¾ cup medium grain bulgur

½ teaspoon salt

¼ teaspoon black pepper

1. Heat oil in large nonstick skillet over medium heat until hot. Add onion; cook about 8 minutes, stirring frequently or until softened and lightly browned. Add garlic; cook and stir 1 minute. Add kale; cook and stir about 1 minute or until kale is wilted.

2. Stir in broth, bulgur, salt and pepper. Bring to a boil. Reduce and simmer 12 minutes, covered, or until liquid is absorbed and bulgur is tender.

# BUCKWHEAT WITH ZUCCHINI AND MUSHROOMS

**MAKES 6 SERVINGS**

1½ to 2 tablespoons olive oil

1 cup sliced mushrooms

1 medium zucchini, cut into ½-inch pieces

1 medium onion, chopped

1 clove garlic, minced

¾ cup buckwheat

¼ teaspoon dried thyme

¼ teaspoon salt

⅛ teaspoon black pepper

1¼ cups vegetable broth

Lemon wedges (optional)

**1.** Heat oil in large nonstick skillet over medium heat. Add mushrooms, zucchini, onion and garlic. Cook and stir 7 to 10 minutes or until vegetables are tender. Add buckwheat, thyme, salt and pepper; cook and stir 2 minutes.

**2.** Add broth; bring to a boil. Cover; reduce heat to low. Cook 10 to 13 minutes or until liquid is absorbed and buckwheat is tender. Remove from heat; let stand, covered, 5 minutes. Serve with lemon wedges, if desired.

**TIP:** For a different flavor, add pancetta to this dish. Coarsely chop 4 slices pancetta and cook in medium skillet over medium heat about 5 minutes to render fat. Add 1 tablespoon olive oil, mushrooms, zucchini, onion and garlic. Proceed as directed above.

# PASTA WITH ONIONS AND GOAT CHEESE

**MAKES 8 SERVINGS**

2 teaspoons olive oil

3 to 4 cups thinly sliced sweet onions

¾ cup (3 ounces) crumbled goat cheese

¼ cup fat-free (skim) milk

6 ounces uncooked campanelle or farfalle pasta

1 clove garlic, minced

2 tablespoons dry white wine or vegetable broth

1½ teaspoons chopped fresh sage *or* ½ teaspoon dried sage

½ teaspoon salt

¼ teaspoon black pepper

2 tablespoons chopped toasted walnuts

1. Heat oil in large nonstick skillet over medium heat. Add onions; cook about 20 to 25 minutes or until golden and caramelized, stirring occasionally.

2. Combine goat cheese and milk in small bowl; stir until well blended. Set aside.

3. Cook pasta according to package directions, omitting salt. Drain and set aside.

4. Add garlic to onions in skillet; cook about 3 minutes or until softened. Add wine, sage, salt and pepper; cook until liquid has evaporated. Remove from heat. Add pasta and goat cheese mixture; stir until cheese is melted. Sprinkle with walnuts.

# VEGETARIAN ORZO & FETA BAKE

**MAKES 6 TO 8 SERVINGS**

1 package (16 ounces) uncooked orzo pasta

1 can (about 14 ounces) chopped black olives, drained

2 cloves garlic, minced

1 sheet (24×18 inches) heavy-duty foil, lightly sprayed with nonstick cooking spray

1 can (about 14 ounces) diced Italian-style tomatoes, undrained

1 can (14 ounces) vegetable broth

2 tablespoons olive oil

6 to 8 ounces feta cheese, cut into ½-inch cubes

1. Preheat oven to 450°F.

2. Combine orzo, olives and garlic in medium bowl. Place orzo mixture in center of foil sheet. Fold sides of foil up around orzo mixture, but do not seal.

3. In same bowl, combine tomatoes with juices, broth and oil. Pour over orzo mixture. Top with feta cheese.

4. Double fold sides and ends of foil to seal packet, leaving head space for heat circulation. Place packet on baking sheet.

5. Bake 22 to 24 minutes or until pasta is tender. Remove from oven; let stand 5 minutes. Open packet and transfer contents to serving plates.

# SWEETS & DESSERTS

## APRICOT TARTLETS
MAKES 4 SERVINGS

4 sheets frozen phyllo dough, thawed

1 can (15 ounces) apricot halves in juice (not in syrup), drained

4 tablespoons sugar-free apricot preserves

1 tablespoon powdered sugar

1 teaspoon ground cinnamon

1. Preheat oven to 350°F. Line baking sheet with foil; spray foil with nonstick cooking spray.

2. Place 1 sheet of phyllo dough on work surface; keep remaining sheets covered with plastic wrap and damp towel. Spray phyllo dough with cooking spray. Fold in half to create 8×6-inch rectangle; spray with cooking spray.

3. Place 3 apricot halves, cut side up, in center of phyllo dough. Spread 1 tablespoon preserves over apricots. Fold and pleat about 1 inch of dough around edges to form round tartlet shell. Repeat with remaining ingredients to form three more tartlets. Place on prepared baking sheet.

4. Bake 22 minutes or until golden brown and crisp. Combine powdered sugar and cinnamon in small bowl; sprinkle over tartlets. Serve warm.

TIP: Phyllo dough dries out very quickly and crumbles easily. Keep thawed phyllo dough wrapped or covered until all the ingredients are assembled and you are ready to work with the dough.

# CHERRY-ALMOND CLAFOUTI

MAKES 4 SERVINGS

½ cup slivered almonds,
    toasted*

½ cup powdered sugar

⅔ cup all-purpose flour

⅔ cup granulated sugar

¼ teaspoon salt

½ cup (1 stick) cold butter, cut
    into pieces

⅔ cup milk

2 eggs

½ teaspoon vanilla

1 cup fresh cherries, pitted
    and quartered

*To toast almonds, spread in
single layer on baking sheet.
Bake in preheated 350°F oven 8 to
10 minutes or until golden brown,
stirring frequently.

1. Preheat oven to 350°F. Spray four (6-ounce) ramekins with nonstick cooking spray; place on baking sheet.

2. Process almonds in food processor until coarsely ground. Add powdered sugar; pulse until well blended. Add flour, granulated sugar and salt. Pulse until well blended. Gradually add butter through feed tube, pulsing just until blended.

3. Combine milk, eggs and vanilla in small bowl. With food processor running, gradually add milk mixture to almond mixture. Process until blended. Remove blade from food processor; gently stir in cherries.

4. Divide batter among prepared ramekins. Bake about 50 minutes or until tops and sides are puffy and golden. Let cool 5 to 10 minutes.

NOTE: Clafouti is a traditional French dessert made by layering a sweet batter over fresh fruit. The result is a rich dessert with a cake-like topping and a pudding-like center.

# EASY ORANGE CAKE

MAKES ABOUT 6 SERVINGS

1½ cups all-purpose flour

1 cup granulated sugar

Grated peel of 1 orange

1 teaspoon baking soda

¼ teaspoon salt

1 cup orange juice

5 tablespoons vegetable oil

Orange No-Butter Buttercream Frosting (recipe follows)

Candied orange peel (optional)

1. Preheat oven to 350°F. Spray 9-inch round cake pan with nonstick cooking spray.

2. Combine flour, granulated sugar, orange peel, baking soda and salt in medium bowl. Combine orange juice and oil in small bowl or measuring cup. Add to flour mixture; stir until smooth. Spread batter in prepared pan.

3. Bake 30 minutes or until toothpick inserted into center comes out clean. Cool cake in pan 15 minutes; remove to wire rack to cool completely.

4. Meanwhile, prepare Orange No-Butter Buttercream Frosting. Frost cake; garnish with candied orange peel.

# ORANGE NO-BUTTER BUTTERCREAM FROSTING

½ cup (1 stick) dairy-free margarine (not spread)

2 teaspoons grated orange peel

2 tablespoons orange juice

1 teaspoon vanilla

4 cups powdered sugar

4 to 6 tablespoons soy creamer

1. Beat margarine in medium bowl with electric mixer at medium speed until light and fluffy. Beat in orange peel, orange juice and vanilla.

2. Gradually beat in powdered sugar. Beat in soy creamer by tablespoonfuls until spreading consistency is reached.

# GLAZED PLUM PASTRY

MAKES 20 SERVINGS

3 tablespoons sucralose-sugar blend, divided

2 tablespoons all-purpose flour

1 package (about 17 ounces) frozen puff pastry sheets, thawed

8 plums (about 2 pounds)

¼ teaspoon ground cinnamon

⅓ cup sugar-free apricot preserves

1. Preheat oven to 400°F. Line 18×12-inch baking sheet with parchment paper. Combine 2 tablespoons sucralose-sugar blend and flour in small bowl.

2. Unfold pastry sheets on prepared baking sheet. Place pastry sheets side by side so fold lines are parallel to length of baking sheet. Arrange sheets so they overlap ½ inch in center. Press center seam firmly to seal. Trim ends so pastry fits on baking sheet. Prick entire surface of pastry with fork.

3. Sprinkle flour mixture evenly over pastry to within ½ inch of edges. Bake 12 to 15 minutes or until pastry is slightly puffed and golden.

4. Cut plums in half lengthwise; remove pits. Cut crosswise into ⅛-inch-thick slices. Arrange slices slightly overlapping in five rows down length of pastry. Combine remaining 1 tablespoon sucralose-sugar blend and cinnamon in small bowl; sprinkle evenly over plums.

5. Bake 15 minutes or until plums are tender and pastry is browned. Remove to wire rack.

6. Microwave preserves in small microwavable bowl on HIGH 30 to 40 seconds or until melted. Brush preserves over plums. Cool 10 to 15 minutes before serving.

# CITRUS OLIVE OIL CAKE

MAKES 10 SERVINGS

1¾ cups all-purpose flour

1½ cups sugar

1 teaspoon salt

½ teaspoon baking powder

½ teaspoon baking soda

1 cup extra virgin olive oil

1 cup buttermilk

3 eggs

Grated peel and juice of
1 orange

Grated peel and juice of
1 lemon

## ORANGE SYRUP

¾ cup orange juice

2 tablespoons sugar

Orange peel strips
(optional)

1. Preheat oven to 350°F. Line bottom of 9-inch round baking pan with parchment paper. Spray pan and parchment with nonstick cooking spray or brush with olive oil.

2. Combine flour, 1½ cups sugar, salt, baking powder and baking soda in large bowl; whisk until well blended. Combine oil, buttermilk, eggs, orange peel and juice and lemon peel and juice in medium bowl; whisk until well blended. Add to flour mixture; mix until blended. Pour into prepared pan.

3. Bake 40 minutes or until top is firm and golden brown and toothpick inserted into center comes out clean. Cool completely in pan on wire rack. Run thin knife around edge of cake to loosen; invert onto serving plate and peel off parchment.

4. Meanwhile, combine ¾ cup orange juice and 2 tablespoons sugar in small saucepan; bring to a boil over medium-high heat. Reduce heat to medium; cook 10 to 12 minutes or until mixture thickens and is reduced to about ¼ cup. Cool slightly. Pour syrup over cake; cool completely before serving. Garnish with additional orange peel strips, if desired.

# ORANGE GRANITA

MAKES 6 SERVINGS

6 small Valencia or blood
  oranges

¼ cup sugar

¼ cup water

⅛ teaspoon ground
  cinnamon

1. Cut oranges in half; squeeze juice into medium bowl and reserve empty shells. Strain juice to remove seeds, if necessary. Combine sugar and water in small microwavable bowl; cook on HIGH 30 seconds to 1 minute or until sugar is dissolved. Stir sugar mixture and cinnamon into juice.

2. Pour juice mixture into shallow 9-inch pan. Cover and place on flat surface in freezer. After 1 to 2 hours when ice crystals form at edges, stir with fork. Stir 2 or 3 more times at 20 to 30 minute intervals until texture of granita is like icy snow.

3. Scoop granita into orange shells to serve.

EXTRAS: Add a small amount of orange liqueur to the orange juice mixture before freezing. Top with whipped cream and a candied orange slice.

# BAKLAVA

MAKES ABOUT 32 PIECES

- 4 cups walnuts, shelled pistachio nuts and/or slivered almonds (1 pound)
- 1¼ cups sugar, divided
- 2 teaspoons ground cinnamon
- ¼ teaspoon ground cloves
- 1 cup (2 sticks) butter, melted
- 1 package (16 ounces) frozen phyllo dough (about 20 sheets), thawed
- 1½ cups water
- ¾ cup honey
- 2 (2-inch-long) strips lemon peel
- 1 tablespoon fresh lemon juice
- 1 cinnamon stick
- 3 whole cloves

1. Place half of walnuts in food processor. Pulse until nuts are finely chopped, but not pasty. Transfer to large bowl; repeat with remaining nuts. Add ½ cup sugar, ground cinnamon and ground cloves to nuts; mix well.

2. Preheat oven to 325°F. Brush 13×9-inch baking dish with some of melted butter or line with foil, leaving overhang on two sides for easy removal. Unroll phyllo dough and place on large sheet of waxed paper. Trim phyllo sheets to 13×9 inches. Cover phyllo with plastic wrap and damp, clean kitchen towel to prevent drying out.

3. Place 1 phyllo sheet in bottom of dish, folding in edges if too long; brush with butter. Repeat with 7 additional phyllo sheets, brushing each sheet with butter as it is layered. Sprinkle about ½ cup nut mixture evenly over layered phyllo. Top nuts with 3 additional sheets of phyllo, brushing each sheet with butter. Sprinkle with ½ cup nut mixture. Repeat layering and brushing of 3 phyllo sheets with ½ cup nut mixture two more times. Top final layer of nut mixture with remaining phyllo sheets, brushing each sheet with butter.

4. Score baklava lengthwise into four equal sections, then cut diagonally at 1½-inch intervals to form diamond shapes. Sprinkle top lightly with water to prevent top phyllo layers from curling up during baking. Bake 50 to 60 minutes or until golden brown.

5. Meanwhile, combine 1½ cups water, remaining ¾ cup sugar, honey, lemon peel, lemon juice, cinnamon stick and whole cloves in medium saucepan; bring to a boil over high heat. Reduce heat to low; simmer 15 minutes. Strain hot syrup; drizzle evenly over hot baklava. Cool completely in baking dish on wire rack. Cut into pieces along score lines.

# FIGS POACHED IN RED WINE

MAKES 4 SERVINGS

2 cups dry red wine

1 cup packed brown sugar

2 (3-inch) cinnamon sticks

1 teaspoon finely grated orange peel

12 dried Calimyrna or Mediterranean figs (about 6 ounces)

4 tablespoons whipping cream (optional)

### SLOW COOKER DIRECTIONS

**1.** Stir together wine, brown sugar, cinnamon sticks, orange peel and figs in 2- to 4½-quart slow cooker. Cover and cook on LOW for 5 to 6 hours or on HIGH 4 to 5 hours.

**2.** Remove and discard cinnamon sticks. To serve, spoon some figs and syrup into serving dish. Top with spoonful of cream. May be served warm or cold.

## PASTA, RICE & GRAINS

# METRIC CONVERSION CHART

## VOLUME MEASUREMENTS (dry)

1/8 teaspoon = 0.5 mL
1/4 teaspoon = 1 mL
1/2 teaspoon = 2 mL
3/4 teaspoon = 4 mL
1 teaspoon = 5 mL
1 tablespoon = 15 mL
2 tablespoons = 30 mL
1/4 cup = 60 mL
1/3 cup = 75 mL
1/2 cup = 125 mL
2/3 cup = 150 mL
3/4 cup = 175 mL
1 cup = 250 mL
2 cups = 1 pint = 500 mL
3 cups = 750 mL
4 cups = 1 quart = 1 L

## VOLUME MEASUREMENTS (fluid)

1 fluid ounce (2 tablespoons) = 30 mL
4 fluid ounces (1/2 cup) = 125 mL
8 fluid ounces (1 cup) = 250 mL
12 fluid ounces (1 1/2 cups) = 375 mL
16 fluid ounces (2 cups) = 500 mL

## WEIGHTS (mass)

1/2 ounce = 15 g
1 ounce = 30 g
3 ounces = 90 g
4 ounces = 120 g
8 ounces = 225 g
10 ounces = 285 g
12 ounces = 360 g
16 ounces = 1 pound = 450 g

## DIMENSIONS

1/16 inch = 2 mm
1/8 inch = 3 mm
1/4 inch = 6 mm
1/2 inch = 1.5 cm
3/4 inch = 2 cm
1 inch = 2.5 cm

## OVEN TEMPERATURES

250°F = 120°C
275°F = 140°C
300°F = 150°C
325°F = 160°C
350°F = 180°C
375°F = 190°C
400°F = 200°C
425°F = 220°C
450°F = 230°C

## BAKING PAN SIZES

| Utensil | Size in Inches/Quarts | Metric Volume | Size in Centimeters |
|---|---|---|---|
| Baking or Cake Pan (square or rectangular) | 8×8×2 | 2 L | 20×20×5 |
| | 9×9×2 | 2.5 L | 23×23×5 |
| | 12×8×2 | 3 L | 30×20×5 |
| | 13×9×2 | 3.5 L | 33×23×5 |
| Loaf Pan | 8×4×3 | 1.5 L | 20×10×7 |
| | 9×5×3 | 2 L | 23×13×7 |
| Round Layer Cake Pan | 8×1½ | 1.2 L | 20×4 |
| | 9×1½ | 1.5 L | 23×4 |
| Pie Plate | 8×1¼ | 750 mL | 20×3 |
| | 9×1¼ | 1 L | 23×3 |
| Baking Dish or Casserole | 1 quart | 1 L | — |
| | 1½ quart | 1.5 L | — |
| | 2 quart | 2 L | — |